The Woodlands Orchids

Frederick Boyle

The Woodlands Orchids

Copyright © 2022 Indo-European Publishing

The present edition is a reproduction of previous publication of this classic work. Minor typographical errors may have been corrected without note; however, for an authentic reading experience the spelling, punctuation, and capitalization have been retained from the original text.

ISBN: 978-1-64439-580-6

CONTENTS

This work is not of the class which needs a Preface. But to the Editors of the Pall Mall Gazette, Sunday Times, Black and White, Chambers's Journal, Wide Wide World, and Badminton Magazine I am indebted for license to republish my stories of Orchid-seeking, and it is pleasant to acknowledge their courtesy. If those tales amuse the general reader, I trust that other portions of the work will be found not uninteresting, nor even unprofitable, by orchid-growers. Plain descriptions of scarce species and varieties are not readily accessible. A mere list of the hybrids in the Woodlands collection would be found useful, pending the issue of that international catalogue which must be undertaken shortly; but beyond this I have noted the peculiarities of colour and form in such of the progeny as seemed most curious. No doubt many experts will wish that I had described some which are passed over and omitted some described—without agreeing among themselves in either case perhaps. But I have done my best.

HOW THE COLLECTION WAS FORMED

This question may be answered shortly; it was formed—at least the beginning of it—under compulsion. After fifteen years of very hard work, Mr. Measures broke down. The doctor prescribed a long rest, and insisted on it; but the patient was equally determined not to risk the career just opening, with an assurance of success, by taking a twelve-months' holiday. Reluctantly the doctor sought an alternative. Yachting he proposed—hunting—shooting; at length, in despair, horse-racing! Zealously and conscientiously undertaken, that pursuit yields a good deal of employment for the mind. And one who follows it up and down the country must needs spend several hours a day in the open air. Such was the argument; we may suspect that the good man had a sporting turn and hoped to get valuable tips from a grateful client.

But nothing would suit. After days of cogitation, at his wits' end, the doctor conceived an idea which might have occurred to some at the outset. 'Take a house in the suburbs,' he advised, 'with a large garden. Cultivate some special variety of plant and make a study of it.' This commended itself. As a boy Mr. Measures loved gardening. In the Lincolnshire hamlet where he was born, the vicar took pride in his roses and things, as is the wont of vicars who belong to the honest old school. It was an hereditary taste with the Measures' kin. Forthwith a house, with seven acres of land about it, was purchased at Streatham—'The Woodlands,' destined to win renown in the annals of Orchidology.

But the special variety of plant had still to be selected. It was to be something with a flower, as Mr. Measures understood; hardy, and so interesting in some way, no matter what, that a busy man could find distraction in studying it. Such conditions are not difficult for one willing to spend hours over the microscope; but in that case, if the mind were relieved, the body would suffer. At the present day orchids would suggest themselves at once; but twenty or twenty-five years ago they were not so familiar to the public at large. One friend proposed roses, another carnations, a third chrysanthemums, and a fourth, fifth, and sixth proposed chrysanthemums, carnations, and roses. Though the house and the large garden had been provided, Mr. Measures did not see his way.

I am tempted to quote some remarks of my own, published in October 1892. 'I sometimes think that orchids were designed at their inception to comfort the elect of human beings in this anxious age—the elect, I say, among whom the rich may or may not be

1

included. Consider! To generate them must needs have been the latest "act of creation," as the ancient formula goes—in the realm of plants and flowers at least. The world was old already when orchids took place therein; for they could not have lived in those ages which preceded the modern order. Doubtless this family sprang from some earlier and simpler organisation, like all else. But the Duke of Argyll's famous argument against the "Origin of Man" applies here: that organisation could not have been an orchid. Its anatomy forbids fertilisation by wind, or even, one may say, by accident. Insects are necessary; in many cases insects of peculiar structure. Great was the diversion of the foolish—eminent savants may be very foolish indeed—when Darwin pronounced that if a certain moth, which he had never seen nor heard of, were to die out in Madagascar, the noblest of the Angraecums must cease to exist. To the present day no one has seen or heard of that moth, but the humour of the assertion is worn out. Only admiring wonder remains, for we know now that the induction is unassailable. Upon such chances does the life of an orchid depend. It follows that insects must have been well established before those plants came into being; and insects in their turn could not live until the earth had long "borne fruit after its kind."

'But from the beginning of things until this century, until this generation, one might almost say—civilised man could not enjoy the boon.... We may fancy the delight of the Greeks and the rivalry of millionaires at Rome had these flowers been known. "The Ancients" were by no means unskilful in horticulture—witness that astonishing report of the display at the coronation of Ptolemy Philadelphus, given by Athenaeus. But of course they could not have known how to begin growing orchids, even though they obtained them—I speak of epiphytes and foreign species, naturally. From the date of the Creation—which we need not fix—till the end of the Eighteenth Century, ships were not fast enough to convey them alive; a fact not deplorable since they would have been killed forthwith on landing.

'... So I return to the argument. It has been seen that orchids are the latest and most finished work of the Creator; that the blessing was withheld from civilised man until, step by step, he gained the conditions necessary to receive it. Order and commerce in the first place; mechanical invention next, such as swift ships and easy communications; glass-houses, and a means of heating them which could be regulated with precision and maintained with no excessive care; knowledge both scientific and practical; the enthusiasm of wealthy men; the thoughtful and patient labour of skilled servants—all these were needed to secure for us the delights

2

of orchid culture. What boon granted to mankind stands in like case? I think of none. Is it unreasonable then to believe, as was said, that orchids were designed at their inception to comfort the elect in this anxious age?'[1]

Mr. Measures, however, was quite unconscious of his opportunities. It was mere chance which put him on the right track. Tempted by the prospect of obtaining something, forgotten now, in the way of roses or carnations or chrysanthemums, he attended a local sale. Presently some pots of Cypripedium barbatum were put up, in bud and flower. They seemed curious and pretty—he bought them. It was a relief to find that his gardener did not show any surprise or embarrassment at the sight—appeared to be familiar with the abnormal objects indeed. But it would have been subversive of discipline to ask how they were called. So Mr. Measures worked round and round the secret, putting questions— what heat did the things require, what soil, would the green-house already built suit them, and so forth? Finally, in talking, the gardener pronounced the name—Cypripedium. Planting this long word deep and firm in his memory Mr. Measures hurried to the house, looked it out in the multitudinous books on gardening already stored there, and discovered that Cypripedium is an orchid. Pursuing the investigation further, he learned that orchids are the choicest of flowers, that several thousand species of them, all beautiful and different, may be cultivated, that some are easy and some difficult. It dawned upon him then that this might well be the special variety of plant which would answer his purpose.

But he was not the man to choose a hobby without grave deliberation and experiment. The very next essay, only three days afterwards, suggested a doubt. He saw a plant of Dendrobium thyrsiflorum in flower, and carried it home in a whirl of astonishment and delight; but next morning every bloom had faded, and the gardener assured him that no more could be expected for twelve months. This was a damper. Evidently a prudent person should think twice before accumulating plants which flower but once a year, and then last only four days. But just at that time, by good fortune, he made acquaintance with Mr. Godseff who, in short, explained things—not too hastily, but in a long course of instruction. And so, making sure of every step as he advanced, Mr. Measures gradually formed the Woodlands collection.

---

[1] It seems not unlikely that scholars may read this and misunderstand. I am not ignorant that 'the Ancients' had frames, probably warmed green-houses—since they flowered roses at mid-winter—and certainly conservatories. But these facts do not bear upon the argument.

Perhaps it would be logical to describe the arrangement of our treasures. But an account which might be useful would demand much space, and it could interest very few readers. It may suffice, therefore, to note that there are thirty-one 'houses,' distributed in nine groups, or detached buildings. All through, the health and happiness of the plants are consulted in the first place, the convenience of visitors in the second, and show not at all; which is to say that the roofs are low, and the paths allow two persons to walk abreast in comfort but no more.

The charge of these thirty-one houses is committed to Mr. J. Coles, with thirteen subordinates regularly employed. Mr. Coles was bred if not born among orchids, when his father had charge of the late Mr. Smee's admirable garden, at Wallington. After rising to the post of Foreman there, he entered the service of Captain Terry, Peterborough House, Fulham, as Foreman of the orchid houses; but two years afterwards this fine collection was dispersed, at Captain Terry's death. Then Mr. Coles went to enlarge his experience in Messrs. Sander's vast establishment at St. Albans. In due time the office of Orchid and Principal Foreman in the Duke of Marlborough's houses was offered to him, and at Blenheim he remained eight years. Thence he proceeded to the Woodlands.

THE CATTLEYA HOUSE

Our Cattleya House is 187 feet long, 24 feet wide; glass screens divide it into seven compartments. The roof, of a single span, is 11 feet high in the centre, 4 feet at the sides.

The compartment we enter first is devoted to Laelia elegans mostly. On the big block of tufa in front, blooms of Cattleya and Laelia are displayed nearly all the year in small tubes among the ferns and moss; for we do not exhaust our plants by leaving the flowers on them when fully open. Scarlet Anthuriums crown the block, and among these, on the bare stone, is a Laelia purpurata, growing strongly, worth observation. For this plant was deadly sick last year, beyond hope of recovery; as an experiment Mr. Coles set it on the tufa, wired down, and forthwith it began to pick up strength. But in fact the species loves to fix itself on limestone when at home in Santa Catarina, as does L. elegans.

It may be desirable to point out that the difference between Cattleyas and Laelias as genera is purely 'botanical'—serious enough in that point of view, but imperceptible to the eye.

A special glory of Woodlands is the collection of L. elegans. In this house, where only the large plants are stored, we count five hundred; seven hundred more are scattered up and down. Nowhere in the world can be seen so many examples of this exquisite variety—certainly not in its birthplace, for there it is very nearly exterminated. In such a multitude, rare developments of form and colour must needs abound, for no orchid is so variable. In fact, elegans is merely a title of convenience, with no scientific value. It dwells—soon we must say it dwelt—in the closest association with Laelia purpurata, Cattleya intermedia, and Cattleya guttata Leopoldii; by the intermingling of these three it was assuredly created. Mr. Rolfe has satisfied himself that the strain of Laelia purpurata is always present. By alliance with Catt. Leopoldii the dark forms were produced; by alliance with Catt. intermedia the white. Since that misty era, of course, cross-fertilisation has continued without ceasing, and the combinations are endless.

Evidently this suggestion is reasonable, but if an unscientific person may venture to say so, it does not appear to be sufficient. Among six flowers of L. elegans five will have sepals and petals more or less rosy, perhaps only a shade, perhaps a tint so deep that it approaches crimson, like Blenheimensis or Turneri. Could one of the three parents named supply this colour? Two of them, indeed, are often rosy; in some rare instances the hue of L. purpurata may

5

be classed as deep rose. But these are such notable exceptions that they would rather suggest a fourth parent, a red Cattleya or Laelia, which has affected not elegans alone but purpurata and intermedia also. Nothing of the sort exists now, I believe, in the island of Santa Catarina. But we are contemplating aeons of time, and changes innumerable may have occurred. The mainland is but a few miles away; once Santa Catarina was attached to it. And there, a short distance to the north, lives Laelia pumila, which might supply the rosy tinge.

Several artificial hybrids of Catt. guttata Leopoldii have been raised. By alliance with Catt. Dowiana it produces Catt. Chamberlainiana; with Catt. superba, Feuillata; with Catt. Hardyana, Fowlerii; with Catt. Loddigesii, Gandii; with Catt. Mendelii, Harrisii; with Laelio-Cattleya Marion, C. H. Harrington; with Catt. quadricolor, Mitchelii; with Catt. Warcewiczii, Atalanta. Catt. Victoria Regina also is assumed to be a natural hybrid of Leopoldii with Catt. labiata. There may be other crosses probably, since no official record of Hybridisation exists as yet. Curiously enough, however, no one seems to have mated Cattleya Leopoldii with Lælia purpurata so far as I can learn. Thus it is not yet proved that L. elegans sprang from that alliance.

But the hybridisers have an opening here not less profitable than interesting. For the natural supply is exhausted—if any stickler for accuracy object that some still arrive every year, they may overhaul their Boswell and make a note. Sir, said his hero, if I declare that there is no fruit in an orchard, I am not to be charged with speaking falsely because a man, examining every tree, finds two apples and three pears—I have not the book at hand to quote the very words. When L. elegans was discovered, in 1847, it must have been plentiful in its native home beyond all other species on record. The first collectors so described it. But that home was a very small island, where it clung to the rocks. Every plant within reach has long since been cleared away; those remaining dwell in perilous places on the cliffs. To gather them a man must be let down from above, or he must risk his life in climbing from below. But under these conditions the process of extermination still proceeds, and in a time to be counted by months it will be complete.

In describing a few of the most precious varieties at Woodlands, I may group them in a manner to display by contrast the striking diversities which an orchid may assume while retaining the essential points that distinguish it from others. One form, however, I must mention here, for it is too common to be classed among peculiarities, yet to my mind its colouring is the softest and most dainty of all. Petal and sepal are 'stone-colour,' warmed, one

6

cannot say even tinged, with crimson. Nature has no hue more delicate or sweeter.

Adonis.—Bright rosy petals—sepals paler—lip and edges of lobes carmine.

F. Sander.—The latest pseudo-bulb measures 2 feet 3 inches—topping the best growth of its native forest by six inches; from base to top of the spike, 4 feet less 1 inch, and as thick as a walking-cane. This grand plant has been in cultivation for three years. The sepals and petals are those of L. e. Turneri; the lip resembles a fine L. purpurata.

The plant next to this, unnamed, has pseudo-bulbs almost as long, but scarcely thicker than straws.

Empress.—A very dark form of Turneri.

Medusa.—Tall, slender pseudo-bulbs—very dark.

Neptune, on the contrary, has pseudo-bulbs short and fat, whilst the colouring is pale.

H. E. Moojen.—Doubtless a natural hybrid with L. purpurata, which takes equally after both parents.

Godseffiana.—Nearly white; the broad lip carmine—lobes of the same hue, widely expanded.

Mrs. F. Sander.—A round flower, very dark rose; sepals and petals dotted all over, as in Cattleya Leopoldii.

Red King.—Yellowish throat. Lip good colour and round, but narrow, without the prolongation of some or the lateral extension of others. Curiously like the shape of L. Perrinii.

Stella.—Dusky rose and similarly spotted, but different in shape—sepals and petals much thinner.

Boadicea.—Sepals and petals deep rose. Long shovel lip crimson-lake.

H. G. Gifkins.—The sepals are palest green, with a rosy tinge; petals pale mauve. The lip, maroon-crimson, spreads out broadly from a neck almost half an inch long, and its deep colour stretches right up the throat.

Mrs. R. H. Measures.—Pure white, even the lip, except a touch of purple-crimson in the centre and slender crimson veins.

L.-C. Harold Measures.—A fine hybrid of L.e. Blenheimensis and Catt. superba splendens, which takes mostly after the former in colouring, the latter in shape. It is a round flower, with a crimson lip immensely broad; two small yellow spots are half concealed beneath the tube. Sepals greenish tawny, petals dull pink with crimson lines.

Sade Lloyd.—A very pretty form. Sepals and petals rosy, tinted with fawn colour. The crimson lip is edged with a delicate white line, as are the lobes, which fold completely over the tube.

Doctor Ryan is distinguished by a very long protruding lip.

Ophelia.—As big and as round as Catt. Mossiae. Tube very thick and wide.

Macfarlanei.—We have two so named. In this grand example the pseudo-bulbs are more than 2 feet high, proportionately thick. Eight or nine flowers on the spike. Sepals and petals glaucous green. Long lip of brightest crimson.

Leucotata.—Sepals and petals white with rosy tips—lip white, saving rosy lines and a rosy stain.

Nyleptha.—Sepals and petals fawn colour, edged with rose. Very wide lip of deepest crimson.

Haematochila.—Sepals stone-colour flushed with pink, petals dusky pink. Lip carmine-purple, rather narrow, shaped like a highly ornamental spade.

Paraleuka.—All snowy white save the carmine lip, the form of which is curiously neat and trim.

Tenebrosa.—In this specially dark variety the tube is long, closely folded, rose-white, with lines of crimson proceeding from the back. As they meet at the lower edge they form a border as deep in hue as the lip. But our darkest elegans, eighteen years in the collection, has not bloomed for six seasons past.

Schilleriana splendens.—Sepals and petals white, with a faintest rosy tinge and a yellow stain on the midrib. Lip long, straight, forked at the tip, liveliest crimson-purple.

Stelzneriana.—Rosy-white. The crimson of the lip does not spread all over but lies in a triangular blotch.

Measuresiana.—Sepals greenish-yellow, the leaf-like petals similar, pink towards the edges, lined with rose. Both spotted at the tip with crimson. The lip is that of Catt. bicolor, short comparatively, straight, and darkest crimson.

Ladymead.—The white sepals and petals have a palest tinge of rose. On the lip are two broad yellow eyes after the fashion of Catt. gigas.

Venus.—Almost white. Petals veined, sepals dotted, with crimson—the underside of both heavily stained. Lip almost fawn-colour at the edges, with veins widening and deepening into crimson at the throat.

Luculenta.—A very pretty hybrid of Messrs. Sander's raising, palest mauve. Lip rather narrow but grand in colour. Shovel-shaped.

Frederico.—A very odd variety—small. The stone-coloured sepals are outlined with rose, the petals with purplish pink. Both are speckled with brown. Lip brightest maroon-crimson, prettily scalloped.

Platychila.—Pale purple. Remarkable for its immense crimson lip.

Luciana.—Green petals, curling strongly towards the tip; petals widening from the stalk like a leaf, pink with a green midrib. The lobes white, narrow, square, and deepest crimson, the lip that of Catt. bicolor.

Monica.—Snow-white. Petals broad, sepals strongly depressed. In the middle of the spreading crimson lip is a patch almost white.

Tautziana.—Sepals mauve, petals violet, somewhat darker, lip almost maroon. It is singular in shape also, forked like a bird's tail.

Blenheimensis.—Sepals and petals rose with a violet tinge; very broad labellum with a distinct neck, emerging from a short tawny tube—carmine in the throat, purplish at the edges.

Macroloba.—The lobes here are white and enormous. Enormous also is the lip, and singularly beautiful, deepest crimson at the throat, with a broad purple margin netted over with crimson lines.

Juno.—This also has a very large white tube. Sepals and petals rosy, rather slender, fine crimson lip.

Matuta.—Large, broad and shapely. Sepals greenish, with a pink tinge, petals rosy-tawny. Tube very short, lip brightest crimson, standing out clear as a flag.

Minerva.—One of the most spreading, but thin. Colour rose, the petals darker. Narrow sepals. Tube white. Lip carmine.

Princess Stephanie.—Sepals bright green, petals slightly green, edged with pale purple, and crimson lines. Bright lip after the model of Catt. bicolor.

Amphion.—A dark variety. The long lip has two eyes like Catt. gigas.

Beatrice.—A hybrid of L.e. Schilleriana and L. purpurata, remarkable for its lip, long and shovel-shaped, nearly the same breadth throughout.

Morreniana.—Sepals dullish red purple—the lower strongly bowed, as are the wide petals of similar hue. The lip spreads on either side of the white tube like the wings of a purple-crimson butterfly.

Mrs. Mahler.—A hybrid—Catt. Leop. × Catt. bicolor. Very small but very pretty. Sepals palest green, petals almost white, tinged with pink at the edges. The shovel-shaped lip pinkish crimson.

Euracheilas.—Sepals dusky stone-colour, edged with pink, petals all dusky pink. Very large but narrow. The maroon-crimson lip extends at right angles from the tube, without any neck.

Schilleriana.—The variety most clearly allied to L. purpurata. White or palest rose of sepal and petal, the latter marked with

9

purplish lines at the base. Lip a grand purple-crimson, fading sharply towards the edges.

Weathersiana.—Sepals palest tawny suffused with rose, petals mauve. The broad lip of fine colour is so strongly indented that it resembles the bipennis of the Amazons.

Euspatha.—Reichenbach suggested that this is a hybrid of L. Boothiana or L. purpurata with some Cattleya—probably intermedia. It is white, with broad, sepals and petals. The tube is open nearly all its length, and the wide lip of crimson, fading to purplish edges, shows scarcely an indentation.

Hallii.—Crimson-purple sepals—petals darker; the lip approaches maroon.

Oweniae.—In this case the sepals and petals—which are leaf-shaped—stand out boldly, straight on end—rosy with mauve shading, more pronounced in the latter; lip round, of a charming carmine.

Incantans.—A very large and stately bloom. Sepals of the tender warm stone so often mentioned, petals broad and waved, of the same colour down the middle, flushing to rosy purple on each side. A fine crimson-velvet lip.

Melanochites is a very symmetrical flower, though not 'compact,' as the phrase goes. All lively rose-lake, the petals a darker tone. The grand broad lip of purple crimson has a pretty yellow blotch on either side beneath the tube. It is sharply forked.

Pyramus.—Sepals of the flushed stone-colour which I, at least, admire so much; but the flush is more conspicuous than usual. Petals clear rose. Lip vivid crimson, with the same yellow blotches under the white tube.

Bella.—The purplish crimson sepals and petals are tipped with buff. Lip shovel-shaped, dark crimson.

Sappho.—Here the pale purple sepals only are tipped with buff, while the petals, which curl over, are rose. The carmine of the lip is very pretty.

Macfarlanei II.—Sepals of the same colour, but greenish, strongly marked with the distinctive spots of Catt. Leopoldii, edged with rose; petals rose, lined with crimson on either side of the white midrib. The long tube opening shows a strongly yellow throat. The labellum is short, but superb in colour.

Myersiana.—A large form. Sepals dusky, tinged with crimson at the edges. Petals softly crimson. Very long tube. The crimson lip has a pale margin, and a pale blotch in the front.

Cleopatra.—One of the very best. Like that above in petal and sepal, but paler. The broad tube, however, is snow-white, saving a touch of magenta-crimson, bright as a ruby, at the tip of the lobes.

And the lip, finely frilled, is all magenta-crimson, with not a mark upon it from throat to edge.

Wolstenholmae.—White, the sepals tinted with purple. Petals broad, with a purple outline. Lip narrow and long, of a colour unique, which may be described as crimson-purple. In the throat are two curious white bars; between them run arching purple lines close set, which, on the outer side of the bars, extend to the edge of the lip. A very remarkable flower.

Eximia.—Also very remarkable—not to say uncanny. The narrow sepals and petals, almost white, have a mottling of rosy mauve along the edges, which looks unwholesome, as if caused by disease. But the long paddle-shaped lip, crimson, changing to purple as it expands, is very fine. It has two pale yellow 'eyes' elongated in an extraordinary manner.

Lord Roberts.—Very handsome and peculiar. The colour of the sepals, strongly folded back, is warm grey, tinged and faintly lined with crimson; this tinge is much more pronounced in the petals. The large tubular lip, finely opened, is uniform crimson-magenta, not so dark as usual.

A LEGEND OF ROEZL

So soon as I began to take interest in orchids I was struck with the number of odd facts and incidents in that field of botany. One gains but a glimpse of them, as a rule, in some record of travel or some scientific treatise; and at an early date it occurred to me that if the stories to which these fragments belong could be recovered, they would prove to be not only curious and interesting but amusing—sometimes terrible. I began to collect, therefore, and in the pages following I offer some of the results.

It is right to begin with a legend of Roezl, if only because his name will often recur; but also he was incomparably the greatest of those able and energetic men who have roamed the savage world in search of new plants for our study and enjoyment. Almost any other mortal who had gone through adventures and experiences such as his in our time would have made a book and a sensation; but the great collector never published anything, I believe, beyond a statement of scientific facts from time to time. This is not the place to deal with his career; I am only telling stories. But it is not to be dismissed without a word.

Roezl will be gratefully remembered so long as science and horticulture survive the triumph of democracy. I have heard it alleged that he discovered eight hundred new species of plant or tree. It is credible. In the memoir published by the Gardeners' Chronicle, which was brief of necessity, fourscore were enumerated, with the addition, here, of 'many others,' there, of 'etc.' Roezl was no specialist. A wise regard for his own interest confined him almost to orchids in the later years. But in his catalogue of achievements I find new lilies, new conifers, fuchsias, agaves, cacti, begonias, saxifrage, dahlias, convolvuli, tropaeolums, tacsonias—a multitude, in fact, beyond reckoning. In one expedition he sent eight tons of orchids to Europe; in another ten tons of cacti, agaves, dion, and orchids! The record of his travels is startling; and it must be observed that Roezl's first aim always was to escape from the beaten track. His journeyings were explorations. Many an Indian tribe never saw a white man before, and some, perhaps, have never seen one since. Mexico was his first hunting-ground, and thither he returned more than once; Cuba the second. Thence he was drawn to the Rocky Mountains, California, and Sierra Nevada. Then in succession he visited Panama, New Granada, Sierra Nevada again, California again, Washington Territory, Panama again, Bonaventura, the Cauca valley, Antioquia, Northern Peru, crossed the Andes, returned to Bonaventura, and thence to Europe. Starting again he searched Colorado Territory, New Mexico, California, the Sierra Madre; worked his way to Caracas, thence through Venezuela, crossed to Cuba, to Vera Cruz, explored the state of Oajaca in Mexico, sailed to Lima, crossed the Andes again to Tarma and Changamaga, back into Southern Peru, wandered as far as the Lake of Titicaca, searched Bolivia, traversed the Snowy Mountains to Yungas, back to Lima and Arica, crossed the Andes a third time, visited Ecuador, and made his way back to the valley of the Cauca. How many thousand miles of journeying this chronicle represents is a problem for laborious youth. And the botanist uses roads, railways, and horses only to get him from one scene of operations to another. He works afoot.

It is good to know that Roezl had his reward. Eighteen years ago he died, full of years and honours, in his native Bohemia. And the Kaiser himself was represented by a high dignitary at the unveiling of his statue in Prague.

The experiences I am about to tell were made in the course of that long march through the woods from La Guayra in Venezuela to Ocaña in New Granada. Among the special trophies of it was Cattleya Roezlii, a variety of Cattleya speciosissima; but I am not aware that the secluded tribe whose habits interested Roezl so much had any immediate connection with this plant. Perhaps before going further it may be well to note that any assertion of the great Collector might be admitted not only as an honest report, but also as a fact which he had verified, so far as was possible. Dr. Johnson was not more careful to speak the whole truth and nothing but the truth.

It was somewhere round the sources of the Amazons that Roezl sojourned for a while in a village of those strange people whom the Spaniards call Pintados—'painted' Indians. Their colour, in fact, is piebald—light brown, dark brown, and a livid tint commonly described as red, in blotches. They are seen occasionally in Guiana, more rarely in Venezuela and Brazil. The colouring is ascribed to disease, rather because it is so hideous and abnormal, perhaps, than for a solid reason. Roezl thought it 'natural.'

He was making his way through those endless forests by compass, with two mestizos from Columbia who had served him on a former journey, and a negro boy. For guides and carriers he depended on the Indians, who passed him from settlement to settlement. It is fitting to observe here that Roezl never carried firearms of any sort at any time—so he used to say. Of great stature and prodigious muscle, utterly fearless, never unprepared, happen what might, he passed forty years in such wandering as I have

13

outlined, and never had occasion to strike a blow. Several times he found himself between contending factions, the armed mobs of Spanish America, and lost everything; many times was he robbed, but never, I believe, assaulted. Nerve and humour protected him. As for the wild Indians, I fancy that they were overawed by his imposing appearance; and especially by an iron hook which occupied the place of his left hand, smashed by an accident.

This system of travelling at leisure from settlement to settlement enabled him to pick up a few necessary words of each language, and to give warning of his approach to the next tribe. The Pintados welcomed him in a quiet fashion—that is, the chiefs did not object when he repaired an empty hut and took possession. It was at the end of a long 'street,' parallel to the river. The rude dwellings were not scattered. Each stood opposite to its fellow across the way, and Roezl noticed a large flat stone in the middle between every pair. Towards nightfall the Indians trooped back from their fields; but all the women and grown girls entered at one end of the village, the men at the other. This was curious. As they marched up, the former dispersed in huts to the right hand, the latter to the left, each sex keeping to its own side of the stones. After depositing their tools the men came out and gathered silently around the strangers' quarters—only very young children ran to and fro. After a time the women reappeared with steaming calabashes, which they bore half across the road, and set, each of them, on the stone before her dwelling. Then they returned. Forthwith the males strolled back, carried the supper to their respective huts, and in due time replaced the empty calabash upon the stone, whence the women removed it.

It will be understood that these strange ceremonies interested Roezl. Evidently the husbands lived on one side of the street, the wives and young children on the other. The moon was full and he watched for hours. After supper the males returned to squat and smoke around his hut, scarcely speaking; but one after another they withdrew presently, each to his own abode. So long as the moonlight enabled Roezl to observe, not one crossed the way. And afterwards he discovered that this is an eternal rule—a husband never enters his wife's dwelling. The separation of the sexes is complete.

Long before satisfying himself on this point Roezl saw enough to convince him that the usages of this secluded people must be well worth study. He remained among them as long as he could, and even made memoranda—the first and only time, I believe, that he kept records other than botanical or scientific. It may be hoped that they survive and will come to light, since his papers are now stored in the museum at Prague. I am dependent on the memory of those whom he amused with curt stories of adventure over pipe and glass on his visits to England. They are many, and they preserve the liveliest remembrance of one to whom Johnson's remarks on the greatest of modern orators are peculiarly applicable. 'If a man were to go by chance at the same time with Burke under a shed to escape a shower, he would say, "This is an extraordinary man."' Unfortunately, it is the most striking observations alone which they recall, with but a vague impression of others.

Every hearer asked, of course, how the race could avoid extinction under such circumstances? But it appears that the separation is only public—an exaggerated prudery, one might describe it, though we may be sure that the sentiment lies infinitely deeper. The sexes work apart, as has been said; after the men have cleared a piece of ground they leave it to the women, and clear another for themselves. But when a youth has a mind to marry, in the first place he builds a hut in the forest. Then he awaits the train of women returning, steps gently among them, and takes the maiden of his fancy by the hand. She throws him off at once if disinclined, and there is an end of it; otherwise she suffers him to lead her a step before freeing herself. Day after day in that case the invitation is repeated, and the maiden takes two steps, then three, until at length she quits the procession entirely and surrenders. There is no ceremony of marriage, but, so far as Roezl could gather, the bond is absolutely sacred; in fact, if we think of it, those conditions of life forbid intrigue. It should be added that the other women and girls studiously ignore these proceedings, and that till the last moment a damsel may change her mind, repulsing the lover favoured hitherto.

A bride remains in the woodland hut for several weeks, not a soul visiting her except the husband. Meantime he builds a 'town house' for himself, and the mother or female relatives build one opposite for his wife. In fixing the stone between them there is a ceremony, as Roezl gathered, but the nature of it he was unable to understand. Though the pair never meet again in public as long as they live, they spend as much time as they please together in the forest. And really, after due consideration, I cannot but think that the system shows remarkable sagacity. Truth compels me to add, however, that Roezl suspected infanticide. We may hope he was mistaken. Why should a people living as do these restrict the number of their children? The battle for existence is not desperate with them apparently, since they till the soil, and their territory, in effect, is boundless. No Indian race of South America feels the pride of caste; if these do, they are a notable exception in that as in other

15

respects. Girls receive no dower; the expense of marriage, as has been seen, is nil. Why should they limit the family? We know that obvious reason does not always guide the savage in his habits. But when a painful fact is not assured we may allow ourselves the comfort of doubting it.

This is all I have been able to collect about a most extraordinary people. My informants do not recollect, if they heard, whether the separation of the sexes was peculiar to this clan or general among the Pintado Indians. In fact, I have nothing more to say about them.

It was here, however, that Roezl met with an adventure which he often told. His hut, as has been mentioned, was the last of the row—a ruin patched up to keep the baggage dry. He always carried a folding tressle and a light board to fix upon it, which made a sort of desk, with a camp-stool to match. One evening he set himself as usual to write labels and memoranda for his herbarium. The description of a curious plant secured that day proved difficult, and darkness had long set in. So absorbed was the enthusiast in dissecting its anatomy that he gave no attention to a loud purr, though conscious of the sound for some moments. At length he raised his eyes. By the open doorway stood a creature whose dusky fur glistened like silk in the lamplight, and great yellow eyes stared into his. It was a black jaguar, rarest and most savage of all felines.

So they remained, staring. Roezl felt his hour had come. He could not have moved a limb; his hair rose and the sweat poured down. The jaguar also kept still, purring louder and louder. Its velvet lips were slightly raised, showing a gleam of the huge fangs. Presently it drew nearer, still purring—came up to the tressle—arched his back like a cat, and pressed against it. Crash fell desk, lamp, specimen box, camp-stool and enthusiast—a clattering overthrow! The servants rushed in. No jaguar was there.

Roezl used to attribute his escape to the practice of never carrying arms. When the brute was approaching, he must have fired had a weapon been handy—no man could resist the impulse. And then, whatever the issue of the shot, he would certainly have died.

THE CATTLEYA HOUSE

With L. elegans are lodged fine examples of Cattleyas gigas and aurea, with some of their varieties; generated, as we may assume, by natural hybridisation. These rank among the supreme treasures of the orchidist, unequalled for size and rarity—perhaps for beauty. To those who have not seen the offspring it might seem impossible that the stately loveliness of the parents could be excelled. But by a very simple process Nature achieves the feat—she combines their charms.

Of Cattleya gigas we have some two hundred specimens. It is the largest of the genus, saving its own hybrids, a native of New Granada, discovered by Warcewicz in 1848. He sent no plants home, and though a few were despatched afterwards, Roezl practically introduced the species in 1870. Conscious of supreme merit, it is far from eager to bloom; but at Woodlands we do not personally feel this drawback.

Of course there are many varieties of Cattleya gigas, for it is truly said that two blooms of orchid exactly alike cannot be found. But I shall mention only two.

Imschootiana is huge even above its fellows, for a flower may be nine inches across; the colour of sepal and petal mauve, with a crimson-purple lip of splendour beyond conception. The golden throat under a crimson-purple tube is lined with bright crimson; the characteristic 'eyes' gamboge, fading to white.

Sanderae.—Some may well think this the loveliest of all its lovely kin. Probably it is a foreign strain, though remote, which gives such supreme softness to the magenta of the lip. On that ground the golden 'eyes' shine forth with an abruptness positively startling. The broad sepals and petals are sweetest rosy-mauve. Even the tube is deep crimson.

Here also is Cattleya bicolor Measuresiana, an exquisite example of a species always charming to my taste. In this instance the sepals and petals are purest and smoothest olive green; the very long shovel-shaped labellum magenta-crimson, outlined and tipped with white.

Of Cattleya aurea again the varieties are many. It was brought from Antioquia, New Granada, by Wallis, in 1868. If crimson and yellow, tastefully disposed, make the most gorgeous combination possible, as all human beings agree, this and its sister Dowiana are the most gorgeous of flowers. The ordinary form of Cattleya aurea is nankin yellow, but in the variety R. H. Measures, sepal and petal are gamboge. The glorious lip, opening wide from the very base, has long brownish blurs descending from the throat, on a golden ground which fades to yellow towards the edge. There are two clear crimson patches in the front, and the margin is clear crimson, whilst the whole expanse is covered with fine stripes of crimson and gold alternately.

We come to the hybrids of these two which, dwelling side by side, have been intermarrying for ages; and their offspring again have intermarried, forming endless combinations. Cattleya Sanderiana was first discovered under circumstances rather odd. One of Messrs. Sander's collectors, Mr. Mau, was hunting for Odontoglossum crispum by Bogota. He came upon a number of Cattleyas—none of them in bloom—and gathered any that came in his way, taking no trouble, nor even mentioning the incident in his letters. In due course he brought them to St. Albans along with his Odontoglossums. Mr. Mau said nothing even while the cases were being unpacked. Apparently he had forgotten them.

'What are these Cattleyas?' asked Mr. Sander, in surprise.

'Oh, I don't know! I found them in the woods.'

Old spikes still remained upon the plants, and bunches of withered rags at the end. Mr. Sander perceived, first, that the flower must be gigantic beyond belief; next, that it was red.

'Go back by next mail!' he cried. 'Search the woods—gather every one!' And Mr. Mau did actually return by next mail.

This was Cattleya Sanderiana—sometimes as much as eleven inches across; in colour, a tender rosy-mauve. The vast lip is almost square, with a throat of gold, lined and netted over with bright crimson. It has the charming 'eyes' of gigas in perfection, and the enormous disc, superbly frilled, is of the liveliest magenta crimson.

Chrysotoxa, another of these wondrous hybrids, 'favours' its aurea parent; with buff-yellow petals and sepals, the lower of which hang in a graceful bunch surrounding the huge lip of dark orange ground, with an edging of maroon-crimson, narrow above, widening to a stately breadth below; the whole closely covered with branching lines of crimson.

Mrs. Fred Hardy is a third—divinely beautiful. White of sepal and petal, with the vast magenta-crimson lip of Hardyana. The glorious effect may be in part imagined.

We have yet a fourth of this amazing group—Trismegistris—most nearly allied to Sanderiana. I have not seen this variety in bloom; it was introduced only three years ago. But the name signifies that it is the quintessence of all. Individual taste may not always allow that claim, but no one disputes that it is at least equal to the finest.

But the thoughtful cannot contemplate these wondrous things with satisfaction unalloyed. Unless some wealthy and intelligent persons in South America undertake to cultivate them in a regular way, it is too probable that in a generation or two they will be utterly lost; for we cannot hope that the specimens in Europe will endure so long, however vigorous they may be at present. Here is the letter which accompanied the last consignment—sad reading, as I think:—

Medellin, January 27, 1896.

Messrs. F. Sander and Co.,

St. Albans.

Gentlemen—I arrived here yesterday from Alba Gumara and received your much honoured letter of November 11, 1895. I shall despatch to-morrow thirty boxes, twelve of which contain the finest of all the aureas, the Monte Coromee form, and eighteen cases contain the grand Sanderiana type, all collected from the spot where these grow mixed, and I shall clear them all out. They are now nearly extinguished in this spot, and this will surely be the last season. I have finished all along the Rio Dagua, where there are no plants left; the last days I remained in that spot the people brought in two or three plants a day and some came back without a single plant. I left my boy with the Señor Altados to explore while I despatched the boxes and get funds, when I shall return for the var. papilio which Altados promised to secure for me, and go on up to the spot called the Parama San Sausa. In the boxes containing the aureas you will find about 300 seedlings which have not flowered; these are from a grove of trees where no plants have previously been gathered from, and where the finest Sanderianas and aureas grow intermingled in one family. These Cattleyas only flower once in a year—that is, from March to the end of July, and both kinds together. Some of the flowers measure upwards of 10 inches—and on a spike you can have nine flowers. I cannot wait in that fearful region longer than the flowering time; the awfully wild aspect of everything and scarcity of wholesome food and help for the work is simply maddening. If I shall find the other orchids you want I do not know. My boy is gone with Altados for the Oncidium. You may believe me that many more of these fine Cattleyas do not exist, and I can, after all, perhaps not find so good as may be in those you will now receive.

19

In the last years I have seen these plants in bloom, when I was so ill with fever, and in no other place can you get such a fine type.

The plants that I planted when I was taken ill no one found; no one has been here, and the plants had grown well and some of them very much rooted.

Trusting that all will arrive in good order, I remain, gentlemen, your very obedient servant,

Carl Johannsen.

CATTLEYA MENDELII

The next division is styled the Mendelii house; more than three hundred large examples of this species—to be accurate and pedantic, it should be called a variety—occupy the centre, a hundred and eighty the stand to right.

Cattleya Mendelii lives in the neighbourhood of Ocaña, New Granada, at an altitude of 3500 feet. It was introduced by Messrs. Backhouse in 1870, and named in honour of Mr. Sam Mendel, a great personage at Manchester in his day. Distinctions of colour are very frequent. Some pronounce it the loveliest of Cattleyas.

Among the noble specimens here, many of them chosen for individual peculiarities, not half a dozen are named; the rest bear only letters showing their class, and certain marks understood by the initiated. It will be a relief when this system, or something like it, becomes general. And the time is not distant; at least, the privilege of granting new names at will must be restricted among those who obey the authorities.

The few plants here which enjoy a special designation are:—

Monica Measures.—Petals rose, with a broad streak of purple down the centre from base to point. Sepals also rose, tipped with purple. Lip of darkest crimson, fringed.

Lily Measures.—A very large flower, white of sepal and petal. On the lip, somewhat pale, as if to show it off, is a splash of purple-crimson, sharply defined.

R. H. Measures.—Sepals and petals tinted with rose. Enormous lip, very dark crimson, fringed.

William Lloyd.—For this I can only repeat the last description, yet the eye perceives a difference not inconsiderable.

Mrs. R. H. Measures.—All white saving the yellow throat and two small touches of purple in the front.

Duke of Marlborough.—This variety moved the great

Reichenbach, as he said, to 'religious admiration.' No doubt it is the grandest of all Mendeliis—which is much to say; very large, perfectly graceful in form, exquisitely frilled. The colour of sepal and petal pink, the throat yellow, the spreading disc magenta-crimson.

The left side of the house is filled with large plants—some two hundred—of Cattleya Schroderae, which the learned recognise as a variety of Cattleya Trianae. It has the great advantage, however, of flowering in April, and thus, when discovered in 1884 by Arnold, collecting for Messrs. Sander, it filled a gap in the succession of Cattleyas. Henceforward the careful amateur might have one variety at least in bloom the year round. Named of course after Baroness Schröder. All Cattleyas are scented more or less at certain times of the day, but none so strongly as this, nor so persistently.

It does not vary so much as most of its kin, but it shows perhaps a greater tendency to albinism than any—as seems natural when its colours are so much paler. Among these grand plants we have three white, notably—

Miss Mary Measures, of which the picture is given.

Overhead hang smaller plants of Cattleya Mossiae, Trianae, Mendelii, and Laelia Lucasiana; among them no less than five Cattleya speciosissima alba.

Speciosissima Dawsonii is here also, finest of the coloured varieties—purplish rose of sepal and petal, lip large, yellow in the upper part, rosy crimson below, with margin finely fringed; and

Laelia pumila marginata.—In its ordinary form L. pumila is one of the loveliest flowers that blow, and admiration is enhanced by surprise when we observe how small and slender is the plant that bears such a handsome bloom. But this rare variety is lovelier still— its broad, rosy-crimson sepals and petals and its superb crimson lip all outlined with white.

CATTLEYA BOWRINGIANA

The third division of the Cattleya house contains, in the centre, some hundreds of Mendeliis; Cattleya Bowringiana on the right hand, Cattleyas Mossiae and Wageneri on the left; all 'specimen' plants, for health and vigour as for size.

Cattleya Bowringiana was imported fifteen years ago from British Honduras, but it has since been found in other parts of Central America. In colour—rosy purple, with deep purple lip, white in the throat—it does not vary much, nor in shape; at least I have not heard of any named varieties. But Cattleya Bowringiana in good health is always a cheering spectacle; its young growths push with such a demonstration of sturdiness—having to rise much beyond the ordinary stature—and its bunch of eight or ten flowers stands so high above the foliage. Nowhere may that pleasant spectacle be enjoyed with more satisfaction than at Woodlands.

CATTLEYA MOSSIAE

Since Cattleya Mossiae was introduced more than two generations ago, and remains perhaps the commonest of the species, I need not describe it. Mrs. Moss of Ottersfoot, by Liverpool, conferred the name in 1856. Love of orchids is a heritage in that family—so is the love of rowing. The lady's grandson, Sir J. Edwardes Moss, now living, was Stroke of the O.U.B.C. and at Eton, as were his father and his uncle. And the ancestral collection of orchids is still maintained.

White Mossiaes are not uncommon, though their exquisite beauty makes them precious in all meanings of the term.

Mrs. R. H. Measures is best of all—a famous variety—white of sepal and petal. Deep and graceful frilling on the lip is always characteristic of this species; it reaches absolute perfection here. The yellow of the throat is much subdued, but purple lines issuing from it spread over all the white lip, with a very curious effect. Purple also is the frilling.

Grandiflora.—Deep rose. Petals very broad, lip immense, finely mottled and veined with purple.

Excelsior.—Blush-rose. Lip rosy purple, with a white margin.

Gilbert Measures.—A superb variety. White with a faint flush. Sepals and petals unusually solid. Lip very widespread, with purple lines and splashes of magenta-purple.

Gigantea.—Biggest of all. Rosy pink. The orange of the enormous lip and the frilling specially fine.

Catt. Wageneri, though granted a specific title, is a variety of Cattleya Mossiae, from Caracas, discovered by Wagener in 1851; white, excepting a yellow blotch on the lip.

From the roof, among a hundred smaller plants of Cattleya, hangs a specimen of Laelia praestans alba, as rare as lovely—all purest white, except the lip of brilliant purple with yellow throat. Like many other orchids from the high lands of Brazil, this will grow equally well in the cool house. It is, in truth, a variety of L. pumila; its normal colour rosy purple.

CATTLEYA GASKELLIANA

The fourth compartment is given up to Cattleya Gaskelliana, a species from Venezuela, not showy, as a rule—though striking exceptions can be found, as here—but always useful. Like Cattleya Schroderae it filled a gap when discovered in 1883, for there was no species at the time which flowered in July. Its normal colour is mauve; the lip has a big yellow blotch and a mottling of purple in the front.

About four hundred plants are accommodated in this house, among them four albinos—one with eight pseudo-bulbs and two flowering growths. But the finest flower is

Miss Clara Measures.—snowy white, of course, but with a lip like Cattleya Mossiae. Among others notable are:—

Dellensis.—A noble variety. Mauve-pink—the petals immensely broad. The great spreading lip has a gamboge throat fading to chrome-yellow, intersected with lines of bright crimson. The crimson of the front is defined as sharply as if by the stroke of a paint-brush.

Godseffiana.—Pale rosy mauve. Petals immense. Lip a curious dusky crimson, with a narrow dusky-yellowish outline.

Duke of Marlborough.—Gigantic. Sepals and petals bright rose; the broad lip has the same dusky outline.

Measuresiana.—Very pale. The crimson of the lip, which is long but comparatively narrow, runs far up the throat, but leaving two clear yellow 'eyes' as distinct as in Cattleya gigas.

Sanderiana.—Pale. The lip, of excellent colour, spreads so suddenly as to form a perfect circle.

Herbertiana.—Mauve. A very compact flower. The bright yellow of the throat extends downwards and to either side of the lip in a very remarkable manner. The dusky margin surrounds a purple-crimson stain, scored with lines of deeper hue.

Woodlandsensis.—Here the same oddity—due to natural hybridisation doubtless—is carried much further. The whole disc of the lip is buff, with only the merest touch of purple on either side the central line, and another, scarcely perceptible, at the tip.

Along the roof hang small plants of Cattleya gigas and others.

FIFTH DIVISION

The fifth division is a resting-place, where one may sit beneath a grand specimen of Kentia Forsteri, surrounded by palms as in a nook of the jungle, to compare notes and talk of orchids. After such refreshment we enter the last compartment.

CATTLEYA TRIANAE

To left here are more Mendeliis, to right more Bowringianas, labiatas, and Trianaes mixed; rows of labiata overhead. Specimen Trianaes occupy the centre—some two hundred.

This again is a species so old and so familiar that I need not describe it. But there is none more variable, and we have some of the most striking diversities here.

Macfarlanei.—An immense flower, white, with the faintest possible flush. The great lip, vivid orange beneath the tube, changes to white above the disc. To this succeeds a blaze of purple-crimson, outlined in two semicircles as clear as brush could draw.

Robert Measures.—Lively mauve. The broad petals have three purple lines at the base and a mottling of purple on either side. Lip not large but of the grandest crimson, darker towards the throat.

Measuresiana.—Petals clear mauve, sepals a paler hue, lip very compact. Its carmine rises far up the throat, surrounding the yellow and white 'eyes' with the happiest effect.

Woodlandsensis.—Sepals and petals lilac flushed. The great lip beautifully striped with rosy magenta.

Tyrianthina takes its name from the Tyrian purple or wine-coloured tips of the petals—a singular development. The labellum shows the same tint, even darker.

Here also I note Catt. Harrisoniae R. H. Measures. It cannot be said that this differs from the normal type in any respect; but one may venture to assert that it is the finest example thereof—at least, a finer could not be. Upon the mauve sepals and petals, much larger than usual and more lively in colour, the great labellum, primrose and gamboge, with mauve tip, stands out superbly. There is no more striking Cattleya than Harrisoniae in this form.

A STORY OF CATTELEYA BOWRINGIANA

No tale hangs upon the discovery of Cattleya Bowringiana, so far as I have heard. A planter named Turkheim sent it from British Honduras to Mr. Bowring of Forest Farm, Windsor, in 1884. The species has a wide range. Mr. Oversluys came upon it in Guatemala very shortly afterwards, and curious incidents followed.

This admirable collector was hunting for Oncidium splendidum, a stately flower not very uncommon once, but long extinct in Europe. No man knew its home, but Mr. Sander, after close inquiry and profound deliberation, resolved that it must be a native of Costa Rica. Thither he despatched Mr. Oversluys, who roamed the wilderness up and down five years, seeking a prize within his grasp all the time, so conspicuous that it escaped notice— as sharp boys select the biggest names upon a map instead of the smallest, to puzzle a comrade. But that is another story.

Irritated and despairing as time went by, but not permitted to abandon the search, the collector found diversion now and again in a gallop through the neighbouring States. And once he pushed as far as Guatemala. All these forays were profitable, of course; such a shrewd and experienced hunter finds game in every forest. But Mr. Oversluys was not equipped for the wholesale business, as one may put it, on these expeditions. They were reconnaissances. In Guatemala, at the moment which interests us, he had only two servants and three mules.

I do not know exactly where he came across Cattleya Bowringiana; it might be anywhere almost, apparently, in the Central American Republics. The species was rare and very precious at the time—to be secured, though in the smallest quantity. When Oversluys came upon it, he threw away the miscellaneous rarities he had collected, hired two more mules—all he could obtain—loaded as many as they could carry of the very finest plants, specimens such as we dare not dream of now, and started for the nearest port, meaning to return for more so soon as he was 'shut of your confounded Oncidium splendidum.' In such disrespectful terms he wrote to St. Albans.

At the house where Oversluys slept one night was a boisterous young Guatemalan, one of the tippling, guitar-strumming, all-round-love-making sort so common in Spanish America. But this youth was an Indian or almost—betrayed by his lank hair and narrow shining eyes. Such a character would seem impossible for one of that blood beyond the confines of Guatemala. But the supremacy of the Indians under Rafael Carrera's despotism has worked a change there. It lasted long enough to train a portentous generation. When a pig-driver of their race conquered and ruled the descendants of the Conquerors as absolutely as a Turkish bashaw of old, Indians might well abandon the timid subservience of their forefathers.

This young fellow insisted upon playing cards with Oversluys, who declined. Then he began to quarrel. But a good-looking daughter of the landlord intervened, and he promptly struck the light guitar. After supper he felt the warmest friendship for Oversluys, and dropped off to sleep while babbling a serenade to the landlord's daughter.

The friendship had not evaporated next morning. Don Hilario—he allowed himself the title and a most aristocratic surname—was returning to his native village, through which Oversluys must pass; there to remain, as he admitted cheerfully, until his friends at the capital had suppressed certain proceedings at law. These friends, it appeared, were dames of high position, and the proceedings related to a serious deficiency in his accounts as clerk in the Financial Department. But it was all great fun. Don Hilario could not think of his appearance in the dock without peals of laughter. No apprehension marred his enjoyment. Those great personages named, of the female sex, would take very good care he was not prosecuted—or they had best look out. In short, we recognise the type of a cynical half-caste Don Juan.

As they journeyed on together, Don Hilario noticed the orchids, which were simply slung across the mules. He knew, of course, that such weeds are valued in Europe; every child in those realms is familiar with collectors nowadays. 'Ah!' said he, 'those are poor things compared with the great bushes on the roof of our church.'

Oversluys was roused at once. Since Roezl made the discovery, fifteen years before, every one had come to know that rarities may be expected on an Indian church. The pious aborigines collect any orchid of exceptional beauty which they notice in the woods and carefully replant it on the sacred building. It was the custom of their heathen forefathers.

'Are there any white ones among them?' Oversluys asked. An albino form of Cattleya Bowringiana had never been heard of, but he thought it might exist. And if so the roof of an Indian church would be the place to look for such a treasure.

'As many white as red! I say, what will you give for a dozen?'

This was a difficult question under any circumstances, since the plants could hardly be flowering then; and there is no difference in

26

growth betwixt the white varieties and the red. Besides, Oversluys had not the very slightest confidence in this youth.

'How will you get them?' he asked.

'Never mind that. Pay me half the money down and I'll bring the plants to-morrow. You know, our Indians are suspicious of collectors. You mustn't be seen in the village.'

That was reasonable enough in one point of view, but preposterous in the other. 'Oh,' said Oversluys, 'I must see the orchids at any risk—that's flat! and I must hear how you mean to work.'

'Why?'

'Because if you take them without the Padre's consent you know as well as I that the Indians will be after me at daylight, and—h'm! There would be work for the doctor! What sort of man is your Padre?'

'A sort of pig, of course,' laughed Don Hilario. 'A fat old boar, ready for the knife. And my knife is ready, too! Patience, friend, patience!' His eyes still laughed, but he made the significant gesture so common in those lands—a sudden stealthy grip of the machete at his waist.

This was not an unimportant revelation. 'You are on bad terms with the Cura?' Oversluys asked.

'Not now. He thinks I have forgotten. It's years ago. I was a boy. But the Castilian never forgets! I will tell you.'

The story was not edifying. It related to a young woman in whom the Cura felt interest. He surprised her in company with Don Hilario and beat the lad.

'Well,' said Oversluys, 'I'm sorry you and the Padre are not friends, because I will have nothing to do with removing orchids from the church unless he bears part in it.'

'But the pig will want all the money.'

'You need not tell him how much I am to give you.'

Don Hilario argued, however, until, finding Oversluys immovable, he grew sulky. The fact is that to strip their church against the Indians' wish would be not a little perilous even though the Cura were implicated; to ignore him would be madness. Collectors have risked it, they say, before and since, but never assuredly unless quite certain that the prize was worth a deadly hazard. In this instance there was no security at all.

As they approached the village Don Hilario brightened up. 'Well,' he said, 'what will you give me?'

Oversluys had no money, but he offered a sum—the amount of which I have not heard—payable in Guatemala city; to be doubled if the orchids should prove white. Don Hilario declined this proposal

27

with oaths; he dared not go to Guatemala city, and he could not trust a friend. The negotiations came to an end. Grumbling and swearing he rode for a while by himself; then fell into silence, and presently rejoined Oversluys quite cheerful. The houses were close by.

'It's a bargain, friend,' he said. 'Your hand! It's a bargain!'

'Good! Now I won't take my mules with the orchids into the village. Can you lead us round to the other side? There is a hut there, I daresay, where I can leave my men and return with you.'

Don Hilario declared that such precautions were unnecessary, but when Oversluys insisted he led the way through by-paths. They did not meet a soul. Upon the edge of a broad savannah beyond was a corral, or enclosure, and a shed, used by the vaqueros for slaughtering, branding, and so forth in the season, empty now. Hundreds of cattle browsed slowly towards the corral, for evening approached and the woods were full of jaguars doubtless. Though unwatched at this time of year, they took refuge nightly in the enclosure. It was just such a spot as Oversluys sought. His men had food, and he told them to remain with the animals. Then he returned with Don Hilario.

It is usual to ask the Cura for lodgings in a strange place; he himself puts up a traveller who can pay. This was a rotund and masterful priest. They found him alighting from his mule, with soutane rolled up to the waist, showing a prodigious breadth of pea-green trousers. He wore a triple string of blue beads round his neck, and flourished a whip of cowhide.

Oversluys looked like a traveller who could pay, and he received a greeting as warm as foreigner can expect; a foreigner in those lands is presumed to be no 'Christian.' They entered the parsonage. Don Hilario was to broach the business, but first Oversluys would satisfy himself that the orchids were worth negotiation. He slipped away.

A glance settled that. The church was a low building of mud, as usual. On either side the doorway, looking down the street, stood an ancient idol, buried to the waist, but still five feet high. The features were battered, but the round eyes, with pupils cut deep in a half circle, glared in hideous threat, and the mouth gaped for blood; no need of an interpreter there—one saw and felt the purpose. But Oversluys was not interested in these familiar objects. He looked up. His comrade had not exaggerated the size of the orchids, at least. They were noble specimens. But as for their colour he could see no trace to guide him.

Don Hilario had gone to greet his parents; it was comparatively late when he returned, but then he got to business forthwith. The

Cura was startled. He showed no indignation, but after pondering declined. Before going further, Oversluys asked whether the orchids were white? Impatiently the Cura replied that he never looked at them—very likely they were. People decked the church with white flowers, and perhaps they got them from the roof. He had other things to think about.

Oversluys guessed that the man was eager to sell but afraid, and fretful accordingly. He raised his price, whilst Don Hilario taunted the Cura with fearing his parishioners. That decided him. Loudly he declared that the church was his own, and consented.

The deed must be done that night. But who would climb the church roof in the dark? Don Hilario was prepared for that difficulty. He knew half a dozen fellows of his own age and stamp who would enjoy the mischief. And he went to collect them.

It was long past midnight when the band appeared—a set of lively young ruffians. So vivacious were they, in fact, though not noisy, and so disrespectful to their pastor as they drank a glass for luck, standing round the board, that Oversluys thought it well to prepare for a 'row.' He slipped out, saddled his mule and tied it by the door.

Then the young Indians filed off in high spirits, chuckling low and nudging one another. The Cura followed to the door, commended them to heaven and stopped. Don Hilario would not have that—he must take his share of the enterprise. The others returned and remonstrated warmly. In short, there was such hubbub, though all in low tones, that Oversluys grew more and more alarmed. The Cura gave way savagely, however, and they started again; but Oversluys kept well behind, leading his mule. It was a dark night, though not dark as in a northern climate. He could follow the little group with his eyes, a blurred mass stealing over the plaza. The church itself was faintly visible a hundred yards away. All remained still and silent. He advanced.

A low wall encircled the church. The Indians did not think it prudent to use the entrance—of which those idols were the gate-posts, as it may be said. Oversluys, reassured, had drawn close enough now to see them creep up to the wall. Suddenly there was a roar! A multitude of figures leapt up the other side of the wall, yelling!

That was 'Boot and Saddle' for Oversluys. Off he set full gallop, for the risk of a broken neck is not worth counting when vengeful Indians are on one's trail. But though all the village must have heard him thudding past, no one pursued. Very extraordinary, but the whole incident was mysterious. After fifteen years' experience the collector—a shrewd man at the beginning—knew Indians well, but he could never explain this adventure. Sometimes he thought it might have been a trick from beginning to end, devised by Don Hilario to get the Cura into a scrape. I have no suggestion to offer, but the little story seems worth note as an illustration of manners.

Oversluys had good reason to remember it. Uncomfortably enough he waited for dawn in the dank wood, holding his mule by the bridle, not daring to advance. As soon as the path could be faintly traced he started, and happily found the corral where his mules and servants had been left. The cattle were streaming out already, bulls in advance. They blocked the gateway, and with the utmost promptitude Oversluys withdrew into the bush. Making his way to the fence he shouted for his mozos—in vain; climbed over with no small difficulty and entered the shed. His mules were safe enough but both mozos had vanished, having found or made friends in the neighbourhood. And all his precious Cattleyas, left defenceless, had been munched or trampled flat by the cattle! He never ceased to mourn that loss.

A STORY OF CATTLEYA MOSSIAE

Since orchids never die, unless by accident, and never cease to grow, there is no limit to the bulk they may attain. Mishap alone cuts their lives short—commonly the fall or the burning of the tree to which they cling. Mr. Burbidge secured one, a Grammatophyllum, 'as big as a Pickford's van,' which a corvée of Dyaks could not lift. Some old collections even in Europe show prodigious monsters; in especial, I am told, that of the Duke of Northumberland at Alnwick. Mr. Astor has two Peristeria elata at Cliveden of which the bulbs are as large as an ostrich egg, and the flower stems rise to a height of nine feet! The most striking instance of the sort I myself have observed, if not quite the biggest, was a Cattleya Mossiae sent home by Mr. Arnold. It enclosed two great branches of a tree, rising from the fork below which it was sawn off—a bristling mass four feet thick and five feet high; two feet more must be added if we reckon the leaves. As for the number of flower-scapes it bore last season, to count them would have been the work of hours; roughly I estimated a thousand, bearing not less than three blooms, each six inches across. Fancy cannot rise to the conception of that gorgeous display. I doubt not that the forest would be scented for a hundred yards round.

Such giant Cattleyas are very rare in the 'wild state.' An orchid, though immortal, is subject to so many accidents that only species of very quick growth attain great age; these are less exposed to the perils of youth, naturally. From time to time, however, an Indian removes some plant which strikes him for its beauty or its size, and starts it afresh on a tree not too tall—and therefore young—in view of his hut. Thus it takes a new lease of life and grows indefinitely. I have not heard that 'white' peons are so aesthetic.

This Cattleya Mossiae had been rescued by an Indian. Mr. Arnold first saw it on his memorable search for Masdevallia Tovarensis. I must tell that episode to begin with.

More than thirty years ago a German resident at Tovar sent a white Masdevallia to a friend in England. There were very few species of the genus, few plants indeed, under cultivation at that time, and all scarlet. The novelty made a vast sensation. For a good many years the owner kept dividing his single specimen, and putting fragments on the market, where they fetched a very long price. Under such circumstances a man is not inclined to tell where his treasure comes from. At an earlier date this gentleman had published the secret so far as the name 'Tovar' went. But there are

31

several places so called in Spanish America, and importers hesitated. At length Mr. Sander made up his mind. He sent Mr. Arnold to Tovar in New Grenada.

Masdevallias are reckoned among the most difficult of orchids to import. From their home in cool uplands they must be transported through some of the hottest regions on the globe, and they have no pseudo-bulbs to sustain them; a leaf and a root, one may say, compose each tiny plant.

Mr. Arnold, therefore, was provided with some sacks of Sphagnum moss in which to stow his finds. These sacks he registered among his personal baggage. At Waterloo, however, the station-master demurred. Moss, said he, must travel by goods train. Arnold had not allowed himself time to spare. The Royal mail steamer would leave within an hour of his arrival at Southampton; to go without his moss was useless; and a pig-headed official refused to pass it! Mr. Arnold does not profess to be meek. He remonstrated with so much energy that the station-master fled the scene. There was just time enough to load up the article in dispute and jump into a carriage, helped by a friendly stranger.

The stranger had showed his friendliness before that. Standing at the open door, he supported Arnold's cause with singular warmth and vociferation. The latter was grateful, of course, and when he learned that his ally was a fellow-passenger to Caracas he expressed the hope that they might share a cabin. There was no difficulty about that. In short, they chummed.

This young man announced himself as Mr. Thompson, a traveller in the hardware line, but he showed an intelligent curiosity about things in general—about orchids, for instance, when he learned that such was Arnold's business. Would it be possible for an ignoramus to make a few pounds that way?—how should he set about it?—which is the class of article most in demand just now, and where is it found? Before the voyage ended, that traveller in the hardware line knew as much about Masdevallia Tovarensis as Arnold could tell him. He bade goodbye aboard ship, for pressing business obliged him to start up country forthwith.

Late in the afternoon Arnold, who was to stay some days at Caracas, met his agent on the Plaza. 'By the bye,' said that gentleman, 'are you aware that Mr. Blank started this morning in the direction of Tovar?'

Now Mr. Blank was a man of substance who began orchid-growing as an amateur, but of late had turned professional.

'Bless me!' cried Arnold, 'is he here?'

The agent stared. 'Why, as I understood, he travelled in the same ship with you.'

Arnold seized him by the wrist, while in his mind's eye he reviewed all the passengers; they were not many. The only one who could possibly be Mr. Blank was—Mr. Thompson!

'Get me a horse, sir!' he sputtered. 'Which way has the villain gone? And a guide—with another horse! I'll pay anything! I'll go with you to hire them! Come along!' Ten minutes afterwards he was on the track, full gallop, stopping only at the hotel to get his pistol.

At a roadside posada, fifteen miles beyond, Mr. Blank was supping in peace. The door opened. Arnold stalked in. He was in that mood of intensest passion when a man's actions are stiff though he trembles—all his muscles rigid with the effort of self-restraint.

Quietly he barred the door and quietly he sat down opposite to Mr. Blank, putting his revolver on the board.

'Get your pistol, sir,' said he, scarcely above a whisper, 'we're going to settle this business.' But Mr. Blank, after a frenzied stare, had withdrawn beneath the table. Arnold hauled him out by the legs, demanding instant combat.

But this was not the man to fight. He preferred to sign a confession and a promise, guaranteed by most impressive oaths, not to revisit those parts for six months. Then Arnold started him back, supperless, in the dark.

It may be added that the gentleman whom I have named Mr. Blank lost his life in 1892, when seeking the habitat of Dendrobium Schröderianum, under circumstances not wholly dissimilar. As in this case he sought to reap where he had not sown. But peace be with him!

Without more adventures Arnold found Masdevallia Tovarensis. Of the first consignment he despatched, forty thousand arrived in good health. This quest completed in shorter time than had been allowed, he looked for another 'job.' One is only embarrassed by the choice in that region. Upon the whole it seemed most judicious to collect Cattleya Mossiae. And Arnold set off for the hunting-grounds.

On this journey he saw the monster I have described. It grew beside the dwelling of an Indian—not properly to be termed a 'hut,' nor a 'house.' The man was a coffee-planter in a very small way. Nothing that Arnold could offer tempted him in the least. His grandfather 'planted' the Cattleya, and from that day it had been a privilege of the family to decorate one portion of the neighbouring church with its flowers when a certain great feast came round. Arnold tried to interest the daughter—a very pretty girl: the Indian type there is distinctly handsome. Then he tried her lover, who seemed willing to exert his influence for the consideration of a real

33

English gun. Arnold could not spare his own; he had no other, and the young Indian would not accept promises. So the matter fell through.

Three years afterwards Arnold was commissioned to seek Cattleya Mossiae again. Not forgetting the giant, he thought it worth while to take a 'real English gun' with him, though doubtless the maiden was a wife long since, and her husband might ask for a more useful present. In due course he reached the spot—a small Indian village in the mountains, some fifteen miles from Caracas. The Cattleya was still there, perched aloft, as big as a hogshead. Arnold's first glance was given to it; then he looked at the owner's hospitable dwelling. It also was still there, but changed. Tidy it had never been, but now it was ruinous. None of the village huts could be seen, standing as they did each in its 'compound'—a bower of palm and plantains, fruit-trees, above all, flowers. Afterwards he perceived that they had all been lately rebuilt.

The old Indian survived, but it was not from him that Arnold learned the story. The Cura told it. There had been a pronunciamiento somewhere in the country, and the Government sent small bodies of troops—pressgangs, in fact—to enlist 'volunteers.' One of these came to the village. The officer in command, a good-looking young man, took up his abode in the Indian's house and presently made it his headquarters, whence to direct the man-hunts. Upon that pretext he stayed several weeks, to the delight of the villagers, who were spared.

But one evening there was an outbreak. The lover rushed along the street, dripping with blood—the officer, his sword drawn, pursuing. He ran into his hut and snatched a gun from the wall. But it was too late; the other cut him down. The day's field work was over—all the Indians had returned. They seized their machetes, yelling vengeance, and attacked the officer. But his soldiers also were close by. They ran up, firing as they ran. Some villagers were killed, more wounded; the place was sacked. Next morning early the detachment moved off. When the fugitives returning counted their loss, the pretty daughter of old José was missing. The dead lay where they fell, and she was not among them.

The Cura, an amiable veteran, did not doubt that she had been carried off by force; was not this girl the most devout and dutiful in the parish? He saddled his mule forthwith and rode into Caracas. The officer had delivered his report, which may be easily imagined. Governments in Spanish America at this day resent any kind of interference from the clergy. Had a layman complained, doubtless there would have been an inquiry; in Venezuela, as elsewhere, maidens are not to be carried off by young aristocrats and no word

34

said. But the authorities simply called on the accused for an explanation, accepted his statement that the girl followed him of her free-will, and recommended him to marry her. This he did, as Arnold ascertained. As for the rest—quien sabe?

These sad events account for the old Indian's behaviour. Arnold found him at home, and with him a young man not to be recognised at first, who proved to be the lover. The muscles of his neck had been severed, causing him to hold his head awry, and a slash had partially disabled his right arm. Arnold was told abruptly that he could not lodge there, and he withdrew. But on a sudden the lover whispered eagerly. They called him back.

'Will you buy the Cattleya?' asked old José.

'How much?'

'Fifty dollars and a good gun.'

'It's a bargain.'

He paid there and then, nor quitted the spot, though very hungry, until his followers had sawn through the branch and lowered its burden to the ground. Carrying his spoil in triumph, suspended on a pole, Arnold sought the Cura's house. There he heard the tale I have unfolded.

Not until evening did the Padre chance to see the giant Cattleya. He was vexed, naturally, since his church lost its accustomed due. But when Arnold told what he had paid for it, the good man was deeply moved. 'Holy Virgin and all saints!' he cried, 'there will be murder!' And he set off running to the Indian's house. It was empty. José and the lover had been seen on the road to Caracas hours before—with the gun.

I am sorry that I cannot finish the story; too often we miss the dénoûment in romances of actual life. But the Cura felt no doubt. It may be to-night, or next year, or ten years hence, he said, but the captain is doomed. Our Indians never forget nor forgive, nor fail when at length they strike.

The murder was not announced whilst Arnold remained in the country. But all whom he questioned gave the same forecast. Unless the Indians were seized or died they would surely have vengeance.

CYPRIPEDIUM INSIGNE

Here is a house full of Cypripedium insigne; nothing else therein save a row of big Cymbidiums in vases down the middle, Odontoglossum citrosmum and Cattleya citrina hanging on wires overhead. Every one knows this commonest of Cypripeds, though many may be unacquainted with the name. Once I looked into a show of window-gardening in the precincts of Westminster Abbey, and among the poor plants there, treasures of the poorest, I found a Cypripedium insigne—very healthy and well-grown too. But when I called the judges' attention, they politely refused to believe me, though none of them could say what the mysterious vegetable was—not the least curious detail of the incident. The flower cannot be called beautiful, but undeniably it is quaint, and the honest unsophisticated public loves it. Moreover the bloom appears in November, lasting till Christmas, if kept quite cool. The species was introduced from Sylhet so long ago as 1820, but it flourishes in many districts on the southern slope of the Himalayas. New habitats are constantly discovered.

There are 505 plants in this house, and if individual flowers be not striking commonly—that is, flowers of the normal type—the spectacle is as pretty as curious when hundreds are open at once, apple-green, speckled with brown and tipped with white. But to my taste, as a 'grower,' the sight is pleasant at all seasons, for the green and glossy leaves encircle each pot so closely that they form a bank of foliage without a gap all round. But besides this house we have one much larger elsewhere, containing no less than 2500 examples of the same species. If no two flowers of an orchid on the same plant be absolutely similar, as experts declare—and I have often proved the rule—one may fancy the sum of variation among three thousand. Individually, however, it is so minute in the bulk of Cypripedium insigne that a careless observer sees no difference among a hundred blooms. I note some of the prominent exceptions.

Clarissimum.—Large, all white, except a greenish tinge at base of the dorsal, and the broad yellow shield of the column.

Laura Kimball, on the other hand, is all ochreous yellow, save the handsome white crown of the dorsal and a narrow white margin descending from it.

Statterianum is much like this, but spotted in the usual way.

Bohnhoffianum has a dorsal of curious shape. The crest rises sharply between square shoulders which fold over, displaying the reverse. It has no spots, but at the base is a chestnut blotch,

36

changing to vivid green, which again vanishes abruptly, leaving a broad white margin. Vivid green also are the petals, with brown lines; the slipper paler. This example is unique.

Macfarlanei is all yellowish green, with a white crest.

Amesiae.—The dorsal has a broad white outline and a drooping crest. To white succeeds a brilliant green, and to that, in the middle, bright chestnut. Chestnut lines also, and dots, mount upward. The green petals are similarly lined, and the slipper is greenish, tinged with chestnut.

Longisepalum is flesh-colour, with a greenish tinge and pink spots on the very long dorsal. The pink spots change to lines upon the petals. Slipper ruddy green.

Dimmockianum.—The broad and handsome dorsal is green, with white margin. A red stain at the base is continued in lines of spots upwards. The petals are scored with the same colour.

Measuresiae.—Big, with a grand dorsal, pale grass-green below, broadly whitening as it swells. Petals the same green, with a dark midrib and fainter lines. Slipper yellow.

Rona is an example of the common type in its utmost perfection—large, symmetrical, its green tinge the liveliest possible, its white both snowy and broad, and its spots so vigorously imprinted that they rise above the surface like splashes of solid chocolate.

Majesticum is another of the same class, but distinguished by the enormous size of its dorsal.

Dorothy.—Dorsal greenish yellow, with faint spots of chestnut and a broad white margin. Petals and slipper the same greenish-yellow tone.

R. H. Measures.—For size as for colour this variety is astonishing. Its gigantic dorsal is white, prettily stained at base with pale green, in which are enormous red spots, irregularly set. Petals tawny greenish, with lines and dots of red. The slipper matches.

Harefield Hall variety resembles this, but smaller. The great spots of the dorsal are more crimson, the petals and slipper a darker hue.

Frederico.—Within a broad white outline the dorsal is all yellow, heavily spotted and splashed with chestnut. The reddish tawny petals are lined and spotted with chestnut, and the tawny slipper shows a chestnut network.

Corrugatum.—The name refers to a peculiarity unique and inexplicable. The slipper, so smooth in every other case, has a strong breastbone, so to say, and five projecting ribs on either side, arching round diagonally from the back—pale brown on a darker

37

ground. The dorsal is all yellow, spotted with brown, but the crest overhangs, showing its white underside.

Drewett's variety.—Dorsal white, with a green base and huge blotches of red-brown; greenish petals lined with the same; ruddy greenish slipper.

Eximium.—A natural hybrid doubtless, though we cannot guess what its other parent may be; it came among a lot of the ordinary form. Very small. The funny little dorsal is yellow, spotted throughout with red. The small petals have a crimson tinge, much darker in the upper length. Slipper dull crimson; the yellow shield of the column is very conspicuous on that ground.

Hector.—The dorsal is pale grass-green, with a white crest and margin and large chestnut spots; petals and slipper reddish ochre.

Punctatum is a title very commonly bestowed when the usual spots run together, making small blotches, arranged in lines; often the petals have a white margin, more or less broad, which shows them off.

Here also I should mention the famous Cyp. ins. Sanderae, though, as a matter of fact, it is lodged elsewhere. The story of this wonderful orchid has often been told, but not every one has heard it. I may be allowed to quote my own version, published in About Orchids—a Chat (Chapman and Hall, 1893). 'Among a great number of Cypripedium insigne received at St. Albans, and "established" there, Mr. Sander noted one presently of which the flower-stalk was yellow instead of brown, as is usual. Sharp eyes are a valuable item of the orchid-growers' stock-in-trade, for the smallest peculiarity among such "sportive" objects should not be neglected. Carefully he put the yellow-stalk aside. In due course the flower opened and proved to be all golden. Mr. Sander cut his plant in two, sold half for seventy-five guineas at Protheroe's auction rooms, and the other half to Mr. R. H. Measures. One of the purchasers divided his plant and sold two bits at a hundred guineas each. Another piece was bought back by Mr. Sander, who wanted it for hybridising, at two hundred and fifty guineas.' Not less than forty exist perhaps at the present time, for as soon as a morsel proves big enough to be divided, divided it is. Here we have two fine plants and a healthy young fragment.

To describe the flower is an ungrateful task. Tints so exquisitely soft are not to be defined in words; it is pleasanter to sum them up in the phrase 'all golden,' as I did formerly, when there was no need for precision. But here I must be specific, and in truth Cypripedium insigne Sanderae is not to be so described. The dorsal, beautifully waved, has a broad white margin and a cloud of the tenderest grass-green in the midst, covered with a soft green network. There are a few tiniest specks of brown on either side the midrib. The petals might be termed palest primrose, but when compared with the pure yellow slipper a pretty tinge of green declares itself. A marvel of daintiness and purity.

In this house hang Catt. citrina, Odont. citrosmum, and Laelia Jongheana—five rows. Of the first, so charming but so common, it is enough to say that the owner of this collection has contrived to secure the very biggest examples, in their native growth, that a sane imagination could conceive—so big that I should not have credited a report of their dimensions. The ordinary form of citrosmum also demands no comment, and I deal with the interesting Laelia Jongheana elsewhere. But we have a number of citrosmum roseum, which has white sepals and petals and a pink lip; of citrosmum album, all purest white, save the yellow crest; and of the cream-coloured variety, which to my mind is loveliest of all. Sir Trevor Lawrence collects these at every opportunity, and I remember the charming display he made once at the Temple Show, when their long pendulous garlands formed the backing to his stand.

STORY OF CATTLEYA SKINNERI ALBA

The annals of botany are full of incident and adventure, especially that branch which deals with orchids. All manner of odd references and associations one finds there. I myself, having studied the subject, was not much surprised to meet with a tale of orchids and cock-fighting lately; but others may like to hear how such an odd connection arose.

The name of the orchid was Cattleya Skinneri alba, one of the rarest and most beautiful we have; the name of the hero, Benedict Roezl, greatest of all collectors. This experience gives some notion of his ready wit, cool daring, and resource. But I could tell some even more characteristic.

It is necessary to say that Cattleya Skinneri tout court—a charming rosy flower—was discovered by Mr. Skinner long before this date—in 1836; but no white Cattleya had yet been heard of.

It was in 1870. Roezl had made a very successful foray in the neighbourhood of Tetonicapan, Guatemala, and with a long train of mules he was descending towards the coast. His head mozo could be trusted; the perils of the road—streams, mud, precipices, and brigands—had been left behind; Roezl, rejoicing in the consciousness of good work well done, pushed on by himself towards the village where they were to spend the night.

He had not been there before, but the road—rather, the trail— was plain enough. Unfortunately it led him, after a while, into a jicara-grove. This tree, which supplies the calabash used throughout Central America, has some very odd peculiarities. Its leaves grow by fours, making a cross, and on that account, doubtless, the Indians esteem it sacred; their pagan forefathers reverenced the cross. The trunks spring at equal distances, as if planted by rule, but such is their natural habit; I have the strongest impression that Mr. Belt found a cause for this eccentricity, but the passage I cannot discover. Thirdly, jicara-trees always stand in a low-lying savannah, across which they are marshalled in lines and 'spaced' like soldiers on parade in open order—at least, I never saw them in another situation. Such spots are damp, and the herbage grows strong; thus the half-wild cattle are drawn thither, and before the wet season comes to an end they have trampled the whole surface, obliterating all signs of a path, if one there be, and confounding the confusion by making tracks innumerable through the jungle round.

Upon such a waste Roezl entered, and he paused forthwith to deliberate. The compass would not help him much, for if it told the direction of the village, the Indian trail which led thither might open to right or left anywhere on the far side of the grove. Travellers in those wilds must follow the beaten course.

At length he took bearings, so as to go straight at least, and rode on. Presently an Indian lad came out from the forest behind him, but stopped at sight of the tall stranger. Roezl shouted—he spoke every patois of Spanish America with equal fluency. The boy advanced at length. He could only talk his native Quiché, but Roezl made out that he was going to the village—sent him ahead, and followed rejoicing. So he crossed the jicara-ground.

But in the forest beyond, it was not easy to keep up with an Indian boy trotting his fastest. In a few minutes the guide had vanished and Roezl hurried along after him. Suddenly a ragged rascal sprang out from the bushes ahead with levelled gun. Roezl glanced back. Two others barred his retreat.

Not unfamiliar with such incidents, he laughed and offered his purse—never well filled. Good humour and wit had carried him through several adventures of the kind without grave annoyance; once in Mexico, when he had not one silver coin to ransom himself, a party of bandits kept him twenty-four hours simply to enjoy his drolleries, and dismissed him with ten dollars—which was a godsend, said Roezl. But these fellows only spoke Quiché, and they were sullen dogs.

The purse did not satisfy them by any means. They made their prisoner dismount and enter the forest, marching behind him. The camp was close by, and here Roezl found his guide, hitched to a tree by the neck. The brigand officer and some of the men talked Spanish, and they appreciated Roezl's 'chaff,' treating him with boisterous familiarity; but they would not hear of letting him go until the Captain's arrival. He sat upon the ground, exchanging jokes with the ruffians, drinking their aguardiente and smoking their best cigars, like a jovial comrade.

Meantime the Indian members of the band were out of the fun, and they attended to business. What they wanted of the lad Roezl did not understand, but when he persisted in refusing they beat him savagely. At length it went so far that Roezl could not bear to hear the poor fellow's cries. Putting the matter humorously, he begged the lieutenant to interfere, and that worthy commanded the Indians to desist.

After an hour or so the Captain appeared, and Roezl's case was put before him; at the same moment, however, the scouts brought in a priest. He had resisted probably, for they had bound and beaten him. Such treatment was novel, doubtless. It had taken all spirit out of the holy man, who walked as humbly as could be till he set eyes on the Captain. Then his courage returned. They were old acquaintances, evidently, and the Padre claimed satisfaction. He did not get it; but the Captain set him free, with apologies. The boy proved to be his servant, and he also was released. Roezl asserted a claim to equal consideration as defender of that youth, and at length it was ungraciously allowed. Remembering, however, that his precious orchids would soon arrive and fall into the brigands' hands, to be smashed in spite probably, he ransomed them by a bill drawn on himself at the capital. Then he rode on to overtake the priest, who was Cura of the village which he sought.

Not prepossessing at all was that ecclesiastic. None of the bandits had a more stupid expression or one less amiable. But Roezl found presently that he had some reason for ill-humour. Six cocks had he taken to a grand match at Tetonicapan the day before—three his own, three belonging to parishioners; and every one was killed! The boy had been sent in advance to break the news.

Cock-fighting is the single amusement of that population, besides drink, of course, and the single interest of its ministers—most of them, at least. This padre could talk of nothing else. It was not a subject that amused Roezl, but he knew something of that as of all else that pertains to life in those countries. The dullest of mortals could not help gathering information about cocks and their ways in a lifetime of travel up and down Spanish America; the most observant, such as this, must needs collect a vast deal of experience. But Roezl was not interested in his companion.

Not, that is, until he reached the village. The Cura had invited him to his house—so to call an adobe building of two rooms, without upper floor. It stood beside the church, hardly less primitive. Roezl glanced at the roof of this structure in passing. It has been mentioned that the Indians have a pleasant custom of removing any orchid they find, notable for size or beauty, to set on the church roof or on trees around it. In the course of his long wanderings Roezl had bought or begged several fine plants from a padre, but only when the man was specially reckless or specially influential with his parishioners. The practice dates from heathen times, and the Indians object to any desecration of their offerings.

It was with curiosity rather than hope, therefore, that Roezl scrutinised the airy garden. There were handsome specimens of Cattleya—Skinneri most frequent, of course—Lycaste, Oncidium, and Masdevallia. They had done blooming mostly, but a belated flower showed here and there. In one big clump he saw something white—looked more closely—paused. The plant was Cattleya Skinneri certainly. How should a white flower be there?

All other collectors, perhaps, at that time, would have passed on, taking it for granted that some weed had rooted itself amid the clump. But for many years Roezl had been preaching that all Cattleyas of red or violent tint, so to class them roughly, must make albino 'sports.' I believe he had not one instance to cite in proof of his theory, which is a commonplace now. A wondrous instinct guided him—the same which predicted that an Odontoglossum of extraordinary character would be found in a province he had never entered, where, years afterwards, the striking Odont. Harryanum was discovered. Men talked of Roezl's odd fancy with respect, but very few heeded it.

He tried various points of view, but nowhere could the flower be seen distinctly. After grumbling and fuming a while the Cura left him, and presently he followed. That reverend person was an object of interest now. At the first opportunity Roezl mentioned that he was seeking a white Flor de San Sebastian, as they name Cattleya Skinneri, for which he would pay a good sum, and asked if there were any in the neighbourhood.

The Cura replied at once, 'You won't get one here. Many years ago my people found one in the forest, but they never saw another before or since.'

'What did they do with it?' Roezl asked breathlessly.

'Fixed it on the church, of course.'

The man was stupid, but in those parts an idiot can see any opening for trade. To suppose that a cock-fighting Guatemalan priest could have scruples about stripping his church would be grotesque. If he did not snatch at the chance to make money, when told that the stranger would pay for his whim, it must be because the removal of that plant would be so hazardous that he did not even think of it. Roezl dropped the subject.

They ate—more especially, they drank. The leading men of the village came in to hear the sad story of the cock-fight. Not one word on any other topic was spoken until they withdrew to bed. But Roezl was not bored after a while. So soon as he grasped the situation, his quick wits began speculating and contriving means to tempt the Padre. And as he listened to the artless if not innocent discourse of these rustics, gradually a notion formed itself.

The issue of the great match had been a disaster all round. In the first place, there was an antique feud with the victors. Secondly, their cocks had been defeated so often that for two years past they had lain low, saving their money to buy champion birds at the capital. And this was the result! In the assurance of triumph they had staked all they could raise upon the issue. That money was lost, and the cocks besides. Utter rout and bankruptcy! No wonder the priest sent his boy ahead to break the awful news.

43

Despairingly they speculated on the causes of their bad luck from year to year, and it was in listening to this discussion that Roezl perceived a gleam of hope. The mules arrived with his orchids, and started again in the morning; but he stayed behind. The Cura was more than willing to explain the local system of feeding, keeping, training, and in general of managing cocks. Roezl went into it thoroughly without comment; but when the leading parishioners assembled at night, as usual, he lifted up his voice.

'My friends,' said he, 'you are always beaten because you do not understand the tricks of these wily townsmen. What you should import from Guatemala is not champion cocks, but a good cockmaster, up to date. I'm afraid he would sell you indeed, but there is no other way.'

They looked at one another astounded, but the Cura broke out, 'Rubbish! What do we do wrong?'

'Only a fool gives away valuable secrets. If you want my information you must pay for it. But I will tell you one thing. You keep your cocks tied up in a cupboard'—I am giving the sense of his observations—'by themselves, where they get spiritless and bored. You have been to Tetonicapan. Is that how they do there? In every house you see the cocks tied in a corner of the living room, where people come and go, often bringing their own birds with them. Hens enter too sometimes. So they are always lively and eager. This you have seen! Is it not so?'

'It is,' they muttered with thoughtful brows.

'Well, I make you a present of that hint. If you want any more valuable, you must pay.' And he withdrew.

Weighty was the consultation doubtless. Presently they went in search of him, the whole body, and asked his terms.

'You shall not buy on speculation,' said Roezl. 'Is there a village in the neighbourhood where they treat their cocks as you do, and could you make a match for next Sunday? Yes? Well, then, you shall tie up your birds in a public room, follow my directions in feeding, and so forth. If you conquer, you shall pay me; if not, not.'

'What shall we pay?' asked the Cura.

'Your reverence and all these caballeros shall swear on the altar to give me the white Flor de San Sebastian which grows on the church roof.'

The end is foreseen. Roezl carried off his White Cattleya and sold it to Mr. George Hardy of Manchester for 280 guineas.

THE PHALAENOPSIS HOUSE

Phalaenopsis are noted for whimsicality. They flourish in holes and corners where no experienced gardener would put them, and they flatly refuse to live under all the conditions most approved by science. Most persons who grow them have such adventures to tell, their own or reported. Sir Trevor Lawrence mentioned at the Orchid Conference that he once built a Phalaenopsis house at the cost of £600; after a few months' trial he restored his plants to their old unsatisfactory quarters and turned this beautiful building to another purpose. The authorities at Kew tell the same story with rueful merriment. In both cases, the situation, the plan, every detail, had been carefully and maturely weighed, with intimate knowledge of the eccentricities to be dealt with and profound respect for them. Upon the other hand, I could name a 'grower' of the highest standing who used to keep his Phalaenopsis in a ramshackle old greenhouse belonging to a rough market-gardener of the neighbourhood—perhaps does still. How he came to learn that they would thrive there as if under a blessed spell I have forgotten. But once I paid the market-gardener a visit and there, with my own eyes, beheld them flourishing under conditions such that I do not expect a plain statement of the facts to be believed. In the midst of the rusty old ruin was a stand with walls of brick; above this wires had been fixed along the roof. The big plants hung lowest. Upon the edges of their baskets smaller plants were poised, and so they stood, one above another, like a child's house of cards—I am afraid to say how high. A labouring man stood first at one end, then at the other, and cheerfully plied the syringe. They were not taken down nor touched from month to month.

Seeing and hearing all this, I cried—but the reader can imagine what I cried.

'Well,' replied the market-gardener, 'I don't understand your orchids. But I shouldn't ha' thought they was looking poorly.'

Poorly! Under these remarkable circumstances some scores of Phalaenopsis were thriving as I never saw them elsewhere.

In this house they do very well, growing and flowering freely, giving no trouble by mysterious ailments. We have most of the large species—amabilis, Stuartiana, Schilleriana, Sanderiana, etc. No description of these is required. Hybrids of Phalaenopsis are few as yet. Here is Hebe, the product of rosea × Sanderiana, rosy white of sepal and petal, bright pink of lip, yellow at the base.

On the left is a 'rockery' of tufa, planted with the hybrid

Anthuriums which Messrs. Sander have been producing so industriously of late years. To my mind, an infant could make flowers as good as Anthuriums, if equipped with a sufficient quantity of sealing-wax, red and pink and white. Their form is clumsy, and grace they have none. But when they recognise a fashion, the wise cease to protest. Anthuriums are the fashion.

Since that is so, and many worthy persons will be interested, I name the hybrids here.

Of the Andreeanum type, raised by crossing its various forms:— Lawrenciae, pure white; Goliath, blood-red; Salmoniae, flesh-colour; Lady Godiva, white faintly tinged with flesh-colour; Albanense, deep red, spadix vermilion—this was one of the twelve 'new plants' which won the First Prize at the International Exhibition 1892.

Of the Rothschildianum type:—Saumon, salmon-colour; niveum, very large, whitish, with orange-red markings; aurantiacum, coloured like the yolk of egg; The Queen, evenly marked in red, orange, and white.

Overhead hang small plants of Phalaenopsis and Dendrobium; on a shelf above the Anthuriums, against the glass, two large specimens of the noble Cyp. bellatulum album—which with a despairing effort I have tried to sketch elsewhere—and no less than 380 plants of Cyp. Godefroyae, and its variety, Cyp. leucochilum, both white, heavily spotted with brownish purple.

THE VANDA HOUSE

Lies beyond. Only the tall species are here, for such gems as V. Kimballiana and Amesiana would be lost among these giants. But there is little to say about our Vandas beyond a general commendation of their fine stature and glossy leaves. It is not a genus which we study, and the plants belong to ordinary species— the best of their class, however. For the benefit of experts I may mention, among specimens of Vanda suavis, the Dalkeith variety, Rollison's, Veitch's, Wingate, and Manchester; among Vanda tricolor, planilabris—grandest of all—Dalkeith, aurea, Pattison's, insignis, Rohaniana.

But Miss Joaquim must be mentioned (V. teres × V. Hookeriana), sepals and petals of a pretty rose colour, lip orange; a flower charming in itself, but still more notable as the product of a young lady's enthusiasm. Miss Agnes Joaquim is the daughter of a Consul at Singapore, residing at Mount Narcis in the vicinity.

STORY OF VANDA SANDERIANA

There are those who pronounce Vanda Sanderiana the stateliest of all orchids. To compare such numberless and varied forms of beauty is rather childish. But it will be allowed that a first view of those enormous flowers, ten or more upon a stalk—lilac above, pale cinnamon below, covered with a network of crimson lines—is a memorable sensation for the elect.

We may fancy the emotions of Mr. Roebelin on seeing it—the earliest of articulate mortals so favoured. His amazement and delight were not alloyed by anticipation, for no rumour of the marvel had gone forth. Roebelin was travelling 'on spec' for once. In 1879 Mr. Sander learned that the Philippine Government was about to establish a mail service from Manila to Mindanao. Often had he surveyed that great island longingly, from his arm-chair at St. Albans, assured that treasures must await the botanist there. But although the Spaniards had long held settlements upon the coast, and, of course, claimed sovereignty over the whole, there had hitherto been no regular means of communication with a port whence steamers sailed for Europe. A collector would be at the mercy of chance for transmitting his spoil, after spending assuredly a thousand pounds. It was out of the question. But the establishment of a line of steamers to Manila transformed the situation. Forthwith Roebelin was despatched, to find what he could.

He landed, of course, at the capital, Mindanao; and the Spaniards—civil, military, even ecclesiastic—received him cordially. Any visitor was no less than a phenomenon to them. It is a gay and pleasant little town, for these people, having neither means nor opportunity, as a rule, to revisit Europe, make their home in the East. And Roebelin found plenty of good things round the glorious bay of Illana. But he learned with surprise that the Spaniards did not even profess to have authority beyond a narrow strip here and there upon the coast. The interior is occupied by savages, numerous and warlike, Papuan by race, or crossed with the Philippine Malay. Though they are not systematically hostile to white men, Roebelin saw no chance of exploring the country.

Then he heard of a 'red Phalaenopsis,' on the north coast, a legendary wonder, which must have its own chronicle by and by. Seduced especially by this report, Roebelin sailed in a native craft to Surigao, a small but very thriving settlement, which ranks next to the capital. People there were well acquainted with Phalaenopsis, but they knew nothing of a red one; some of them, however, talked in vague ecstasy of an orchid with flowers as big as a dinner-plate to be found on the banks of Lake Magindanao, a vast sheet of water in the middle of the island. They did not agree about the shape, or colour, or anything else relating to it; but such a plant must be well worth collecting anyhow. It was not dangerous to ascend the river, under due precautions, nor to land at certain points of the lake. Such points are inhabited by the Subano tribe, who live in hourly peril from their neighbours the Bagabos, against whom they beg Spanish protection. Accordingly white men are received with enthusiasm.

The expedition, therefore, would be comparatively safe, if a guide and interpreter could be found. And here Roebelin was lucky. A small trader who had debts to collect among the Subanos offered his sampan, with its crew, on reasonable terms, and proposed to go himself. He was the son of a Chinaman from Singapore, by a native wife, and spoke intelligible English. The crew also had mostly some Chinese blood, and Roebelin gathered that they were partners of Sam Choon, his dragoman, in a very small way. The number of Celestials and half-breeds of that stock in Mindanao had already struck him, in comparison with Manila. Presently he learned the reason. The energetic and tenacious Chinaman is hated by all classes of Spaniards—by the clergy because he will not be converted, by the merchants because he intercepts their trade, by the military because he will not endure unlimited oppression, and by the public at large because he is hard-working, thrifty, and successful. He is dangerous, too, when roused by ill-treatment beyond the common, and his secret societies provide machinery for insurrection at a day's notice. But in Mindanao the Chinaman is indispensable. White traders could not live without his assistance. They do not love him the better, but they protect him so far as they may from the priests and the military.

I have no adventures to tell on the journey upwards. It lasted a good many days. Roebelin secured few plants, for this part is inhabited by Bagabos, or some race of their kidney, and Sam Choon would not land in the forest.

At length they reached Lake Magindanao; the day was fine, and they pushed across. But presently small round clouds began to mount over the blue hills. Thicker and thicker they rose. A pleasant wind swelled the surface of the lake, but those clouds far above moved continually faster. Roebelin called attention to them. But the Chinaman is the least weatherwise of mortals. Always intent on his own business or pleasure—the constitution of mind which gives him such immense advantage above all other men in the struggle for existence—he does not notice his surroundings much. Briefly, a tremendous squall caught them in sight of port—one of those sudden outbursts which make fresh-water sailing so perilous in the Tropics. The wind swooped down like a hurricane from every quarter at once, as it seemed. For a moment the lake lay still, hissing, beaten down by the blow; then it rose in solid bulk like waves of the ocean. In a very few minutes the squall passed on; but it had swamped the sampan. They were so near the land, however, that the Subanos, hastening to the rescue, met them half way in the surf, escorted them to shore, laughing and hallooing, and returned to dive for the cargo. It was mostly recovered in time.

These people do not build houses in the water, like so many of their kin. They prefer the safety of high trees; it is not by any means so effectual, but such, they would say, was the custom of their ancestors. At this village the houses were perched not less than fifty feet in air, standing on a solid platform. But if the inhabitants are thus secured against attack, on the other hand—each family living by itself up aloft—an enemy on the ground would be free to conduct his operations at leisure. So the unmarried men and a proportion of the warriors occupy a stout building raised only so far above the soil as to keep out reptiles. Here also the chief sits by day, and public business is done. The visitors were taken thither.

When Roebelin had dried his clothes the afternoon was too far advanced for exploration. The crew of the prau chattered and disputed at the top of their shrill voices as case after case was brought in, dripping, and examined. But Sam Choon found time in the midst of his anxieties to warn Roebelin against quitting the cleared area. 'Bagabos come just now, they say,' he shouted. But the noise and the fuss and the smell were past bearing. Roebelin took his arms and strolled out till supper was ready.

I do not know what he discovered. On returning he found a serious palaver, the savages arguing coolly, the Chinamen raving. Sam Choon rushed up, begging him to act as umpire; and whilst eating his supper Roebelin learned the question in dispute. Sam Choon, as we know, had debts to collect in this village, for cloth and European goods, to be paid in jungle produce—honey, wax, gums, and so forth. The Subanos did not deny their liability—the natural man is absolutely truthful and honest. Nor did they assert that they could not pay. Their contention was simply that the merchandise had been charged at a figure beyond the market rate. Another Chinaman had paid them a visit, and sold the same wares at a lower price. They proposed to return Sam Choon's goods unused, and to pay for anything they could not restore on this reduced scale. It was perfectly just in the abstract, and the natural man does not conceive

49

any other sort of justice. Sam Choon could not dispute that his rival's cloth was equally good; it bore the same trademark, and those keen eyes were as well able to judge of quality as his own. But the trader everywhere has his own code of morals. Those articles for which the Subanos were indebted had been examined, and the price had been discussed, at leisure; an honest man cannot break his word. Such diverse views were not to be reconciled. Roebelin took a practical course. He asked whether it could possibly be worth while to quarrel with these customers for the sake of a very few dollars? At the lower rate there would be a profit of many hundreds per cent. But the Chinaman, threatened with a loss in business, is not to be moved, for a while at least, by demonstrations of prudence.

Meantime the dispute still raged at the Council fire, for the crew also were interested. Suddenly there was a roar. Several of them rushed across to Sam Choon and shouted great news. Roebelin understood afterwards. The caitiff who had undersold them was in the village at that moment! Whilst they jabbered in high excitement another roar burst out. One of the men, handling the rival's cloth, found a private mark—the mark of his 'Hoey.' And it was that to which they all belonged.

The Hoey may be described as a trade guild; but it is much more. Each of these countless associations is attached to one of the great secret societies, generally the T'ien T'i Hung, compared with which, for numbers and power, Freemasonry is but a small concern. By an oath which expressly names father, son, and brother, the initiated swear to kill any of their fellows who shall wrong a member of the Hoey. This unspeakable villain who sold cheap had wronged them all! He must die!

They pressed upon the chief in a body, demanding the traitor. All had arms and brandished them. Probably the savages would not have surrendered a guest on any terms; but this demonstration provoked them. In howling tumult they dispersed, seized their ready weapons, and formed line. The war-cry was not yet raised, but spears were levelled by furious hands. The issue depended on any chance movement. Suddenly from a distance came the blast of a cow-horn—a muffled bellow, but full of threat. The savages paused, turned, and rushed out, shouting. Roebelin caught a word, familiar by this time—'Bagabos.' He followed; but Sam Choon seized his arm. 'They put ranjows,' he said breathlessly. 'You cut foot, you die!' And in the moonlight Roebelin saw boys running hither and thither with an armful of bamboo spikes sharp as knives at each end, which they drove into the earth.

Men unacquainted with the plan of this defence can only stand aside when ranjows are laid down. Roebelin waited with the

Chinamen, tame and quiet enough now. The Subanos had all vanished in the forest, which rose, misty and still, across the clearing. Hours they watched, expecting each moment to hear the yell of savage fight. But no sound reached them. At length a long line of dusky figures emerged, with arms and ornaments sparkling in the moonlight. It was half the warriors returning.

They still showed sullenness towards the Chinamen; but the chief took Roebelin by the hand, led him to the foot of a tree upon which stood the largest house, and smilingly showed him the way up. It was not a pleasant climb. The ladder, a notched trunk, dripped with dew; it was old and rotten besides. Roebelin went up gingerly; the chief returned with a torch to light his steps before he had got half way. But the interior was comfortable enough—far above the mosquito realm anyhow. Roebelin felt that an indefinite number of eyes were watching from the darkness as he made his simple preparations for turning in; but he saw none of them, and heard only a rustling. 'What a day I've had!' he thought, and fell asleep.

It was a roar and a rush like the crack of doom which woke him; shrieking and shouting, clang of things that fell, boom of great waves, and thunder such as mortal never heard dominating all. A multitude of naked bodies stumbled over him and fell, a struggling, screaming heap. In an instant they were gone. He started up, but pitched headlong. The floor rolled elastic as a spring-board. It was black night. Dimly he saw clearer patches where a flying wretch, tossed against the wall of sticks, had broken it down. But the dust veiled them like a curtain. Gasping, on hands and knees, Roebelin sought the doorway. Again and again, even thus, he fell upon his side. And all the while that thundering din resounded. He understood now. It was a great earthquake! At length the doorway was found; holding on cautiously, Roebelin felt for the ladder. It was gone—broken in the rush.

Of the time that followed I do not speak. There were no more shocks. Slowly the sky whitened. He turned over the wreck—not a creature was there, dead or living. Great gaps showed in the floor and in the roof. Through one of these, against the rosy clouds, he saw a wreath of giant flowers, lilac and cinnamon, clinging to the tree above. It was Vanda Sanderiana!

But that plant and the others collected at the same time never reached Europe. Upon returning to Surigao with his treasures, Roebelin found little beyond heaps of rubbish on the site. Earthquakes have a home in Mindanao. But that of 1880 was the most awful on record as yet. Two years later he returned and brought home the prize.

51

STORY OF PHALAENOPSIS SANDERIANA

The discovery of Phalaenopsis Sanderiana was an interesting event; nor for botanists alone. Some thoughtful persons always incline to credit a legend or an assertion current among savages, so long as it deals with facts within the limits of their knowledge. Human beings are truthful by instinct; and if we can assure ourselves that no motive tempts them to falsehood, it is more likely than not that even an improbable story will prove correct. The rule applies in all matters of natural history. Numberless are the reports concerning beasts and birds and reptiles accepted now which were a mock for generations; numberless, also, one must add, are the reports too grotesque for discussion. For imagination asserts itself in the case of animals, and gives a motive, though unconscious, for the wildest inventions. But it is rarely excited by plants. When a savage describes some flower he has seen, the statement may be trusted, 'barring errors'; and they will probably be slight, for his power of observation, and his memory in matters of this sort, are alike wonderful. A collector of plants who knows his business encourages the natives to talk; often enough they give him valuable information. The first hint of Calla Pentlandii, the yellow Egyptian lily or 'arum,' was furnished by a Zulu who came from a great distance to visit a relative in the service of Captain Allison. I may venture to tell secrets which will be common property soon. A blue Calla and a scarlet have been found—both of them on report of Kaffirs.

The story of Phalaenopsis Sanderiana is a striking instance. Its allied species, grandiflora and amabilis, reached Europe in 1836 and 1847 respectively. Their snowy whiteness and graceful habit prepared the world for a burst of enthusiasm when Phalaenopsis Schilleriana, the earliest of the coloured species, was brought from the Philippines in 1860. The Duke of Devonshire paid Messrs. Rollison a hundred guineas for the first plant that flowered. Such a price was startling then. Reported at Manila, it set the Spaniards talking and inquiring. Messrs. Rollison had sent an agent to collect Phalaenopsis there, who presently reported a scarlet species! No one he could find had seen it, but the natives spoke confidently, and he hoped to forward a consignment without delay. But years and years passed. The great firm of Rollison flourished, decayed, and vanished, but that blessed consignment was never shipped.

Other collectors visited the Philippines. They also reported the wonder, on hearsay, and every mail brought them reiterated instructions to find and send it at any cost. Now here, now there, the pursuers hunted it to a corner; but when they closed, it was elsewhere. Meantime the settled islands had been explored gradually. Many fine things escaped attention, as we know at this day; but a flower so conspicuous, so eagerly demanded and described, could not have been missed. As years went by, the red Phalaenopsis became a joke. Interest degenerated into mockery.

As a matter of fact, it is very improbable that the plant had ever been in Manila, or that a white man had beheld it. For it is found only in an islet to the west of Mindanao, the most southerly of the Philippine group. Mindanao itself is not yet explored, much less occupied, though the Spaniards pushed farther and farther inland year by year. Seafaring Tagalas may have visited that islet, and seen the red Phalaenopsis. When they heard, at Manila, how an English duke had paid some fabulous amount for a flower of the same genus, they would naturally mention it. And so the legend grew.

In 1881, a score of years afterwards, the conquest of Mindanao was so far advanced that the Spanish mail steamers called there. When Mr. Sander of St. Albans heard this intelligence he thrilled with hope, as has been told. Mr. Roebelin had instructions, of course, to inquire for the red Phalaenopsis; Mr. Sander's experience teaches him that local rumours should never be disregarded. But the search had been very close and very long. Perhaps there was not another man in Europe who thought it possible that the marvel could exist.

Mr. Roebelin is still living, I believe, and he could tell of some lively adventures on that first visit to Mindanao. Constantly he heard of the red Phalaenopsis; it was en l'air, he wrote, using the expression in two senses. At the northern settlements they directed him south, at the eastern, west, and so round the compass. But he had other matters in hand, and contented himself with inquiries.

I do not learn whether it was accident or information which led him to the little island Davao on his second visit, in 1883. He may have sailed thither on chance, for a traveller is absolutely certain of finding new plants on an untrodden shore in those seas. Anyhow Roebelin knew the quest was over, the riddle solved triumphantly, before landing.

The half-breed Chinaman, Sam Choon, was personally conducting him on this occasion also; he found the vessel (a native prau, of course), boatmen, provisions, and the rest. Everything was at the collector's disposal; but Sam Choon took a cargo of 'notions' on his own account, to trade when opportunity arose.

Davao lies, I understand, some sixty miles from Mindanao. Its inhabitants are Papuan thorough-bred, of the brown variety.

Roebelin was deeply struck with the appearance of the warriors who swarmed to the beach when his intention of landing was understood. A body of men so tall and stalwart can scarcely be found elsewhere, and for graceful carriage or activity they could not be surpassed. A red clout was their only wear, besides ornaments and weapons. They had the kinkled hair of the race (not wool), bleached with lime, and dyed yellow. Very strange and pleasing is the effect of these golden mops, lustrous if not clean, decked with plumes and fresh flowers. But admiration came afterwards. When Roebelin saw the big fellows mustering in haste, armed with spears and bows, stoneheaded maces which the European soldier could scarcely wield, great swords set with sharks' teeth, and outlandish tools of every sort for smashing and tearing, he regarded the spectacle from another point of view. They ran and leapt, brandishing their weapons, halloed and roared and sang, with Papuan vivacity. The vessel approaching was too small to alarm them. Laughter predominated in the uproar. But this was no comfort. Men are cheerful with a feast in view.

Sam Choon, however, kept up his spirits. 'Them chaps make rumpus all time,' he said. 'We see.' He held up a green bough shipped for the purpose. It was all laughter now and gesticulation. Every Papuan tore a branch from the shrubs around and waved it boisterously. 'Them no hurt,' said Sam Choon. 'Good trade.' The Chinaman was as careful of his person as one need be, and experienced in the ways of such people. Roebelin took courage. As they neared the surf, the whole body of islanders rushed towards them, splashed through the shallows whooping, dived beneath the wave, and came up at the vessel's side. Ropes were tossed to them, and they swam back again. But the first yellow head popped up just where Roebelin was seated. Among the feathers twisted in it, draggled now, he saw a spray—surely an Aerides! but bluish-red, unlike any species known. The savage grinned and shouted, whirling the hair like an aureole around his glistening face, threw one brawny arm into the air, and at a stroke reached the bows. Another shot up; another. The sea was peopled in an instant, all grinning and shouting breathlessly, all whirling their golden locks. Among the flowers with which every head was decked, Roebelin saw many Phalaenopsis. And most of them were ruddy!

Sam Choon lay to whilst the islanders swam ashore and formed a chain; then, at a word, they ran up the beach full speed—making a noise, says Roebelin, which reminded him of the earthquake he had lately felt. Simultaneously the crew paddled their hardest, also yelling in the shrill Chinese way. The prau sped like a flash, but half full of water. Beyond the surf a mob seized and carried it ashore.

Papuans have no acquaintance with ceremony. Paying little attention to their chiefs, they are not apt to discriminate among strangers. All alike seized one of these new friends—who brought trade!—-slapped him about the body, and hugged him. Roebelin had been subjected to merciless shampooing occasionally in Indian hammams; but he never felt the like of that welcome. It was massage by machinery.

The women had come on the scene now. Though they took no part, they mingled with the warriors, and showed quite as much assurance as is becoming. But they are not by any means such fine creatures as the men, and they do not allow themselves—or they are not allowed—the curious attraction of yellow hair. Roebelin noticed a few, however, worthy to be helpmates of those superb animals; one girl in especial, nearly six feet high, whose figure was a model, face pleasing and expressive, full of character.

These people live in trees like the Subanos of Mindanao. As soon as his baggage had been taken to the public hall, Roebelin got out beads, wire, and Brummagem jewellery. The glimpse of that Aerides and the assurance of a red Phalaenopsis made him impatient. But even Sam Choon found difficulty in identifying the chiefs, to whom of course presents must be made before business can open. However, the point interesting to Roebelin was settled in an instant. The Phalaenopsis, they said, abounded within a few hundred yards, and the Aerides was common enough. The white man wanted them for medicine? He might have as many as he liked—on due payment. To-morrow the chief would show him, and then a price must be fixed.

He slept in the hall, and at dawn he was more than ready. But early rising is not a virtue of savages. To explore without permission would be dangerous. Gradually the village woke to life. Men descended from their quarters high in air, bathed, made their toilettes, and lounged about, waiting for breakfast. Girls came down for water and returned, whilst their mothers tidied the house. Smoke arose. In due time the men mounted, ate, climbed down, and gathered in the public hall, where Sam Choon was setting out a sample of his wares. Hours passed. But the chief's door remained shut. No one passed out or in.

Roebelin saw people glance upwards with a grave air; but they showed no surprise. He consulted Sam Choon, who had been too busy to notice.

All he said was, "Spect chief get bad bird! Dam! All up this day!' And he stopped his preparations.

So it proved to be—a fowl of black plumage had flown across just as the door was opening. None of the chief's household came down that day. But after negotiation some of the men led Roebelin to see the Phalaenopsis. They grew in thousands over a brook close by, clinging to small trees. He counted twenty-two plants, bearing more than a hundred flowers open, upon a single trunk. Very curious is one point noticed. The Phalaenopsis always grows on the northern side of its support, and always turns its flower spike towards the southern side. It is a very bad species to travel. Of the multitude which Roebelin gathered, not more than a hundred reached Europe alive, and every collector since, I believe, has failed utterly. Very few possessed his knowledge and experience.

That was Phalaenopsis Sanderiana; rather purple than red, but certainly the flower so long sought. With the superb Aerides—now called A. Roebelini—he was even less successful; it is only to be seen in a very few collections of the highest class.

So the legend ends. But there is a funny little sequel. Sam Choon did well with his 'notions.' After Mr. Roebelin's departure, he returned to Davao and opened a promising branch of trade. To secure a permanent footing, he thought it would be judicious to marry a daughter of the chief, and he proposed for the giant beauty whom Roebelin had noticed on landing. The father was astonished and amused, but finally indignant. A Chinaman, however, though thrifty by habit and taste, does not count expense when pleasure or business urge him, and both combined here. The chief wavered, and took counsel of his elders. They also were astonished and indignant; but Sam Choon found means to persuade them. So the young woman received notice that she was to marry the Chinaman next day. Her remarks are not chronicled. But there was much excitement among the bachelors and maidens that evening, and presently a band of stalwart youths entered the hall where Sam Choon sat with the chief—his father-in-law on the morrow. They told the latter gravely that they disapproved of the match. Sam Choon interposed with a statement of the advantages to follow, with equal gravity. Then they threatened to smash every bone in his carcass. So the marriage was broken off, but without ill-feeling on either side.

HYBRID CATTLEYAS AND LAELIAS

To right, in the Vanda House, are many hybrids of Cattleya and Laelia; but we have many more, and it will be convenient to notice them all together in this place. Some have not flowered yet, and therefore have received no name; but even of these it is worth while to give the parentage, seeing that there is no official record of hybridisation as yet. Mr. Rolfe at Kew tries hard to keep pace with the enterprise of enthusiastic amateurs and energetic professionals throughout the world. But comparatively few report to him, and not every one files the Orchid Review. Thus it happens that experiments carried to an issue long ago are continually repeated, in the expectation of producing a novelty. The experimenter indeed loses nothing save the credit he hoped to win. But in the scientific point of view time is wasted and the confusion of names is increased. To contribute in my small way towards an improvement in this state of things I give a list of the Cattleya and Laelia hybrids at Woodlands, long though it be, and uninteresting to the public at large; assured that it will be welcome to those who study this most fascinating subject.

I may take the hybrids as they stand, with no methodical arrangement. L.-C. means the product of a Laelia and a Cattleya, or, somewhat loosely, of a Cattleya and a Laelia. C. × means the product of two Cattleyas; L. × of two Laelias.

L.-C. Ancona (Catt. Harrisoniae × L. purpurata) represents each parent almost equally, taking after Catt. Harrisoniae in colour and size of sepal and petal; in general shape and in the hues of the labellum after L. purpurata.

L.-C. Nysa (L. crispa × Catt. Warcewiczii).—Pale mauve—the petals have a sharp touch of crimson at the tips. Labellum all evenly crimson with a narrow outline of white, gracefully frilled.

L. × Measuresiana.—A natural hybrid, very rare, assumed to be the product of L. elegans × L. purpurata. Rosy mauve. From the tube, very long, the labellum opens squarely, purple, with a clouded throat and dusky yellow 'eyes.'

L.-C. Arnoldiana (L. purpurata × Catt. labiata). Large, clear mauve. Petals much attenuated at the ends, which gives them a sort of 'fly-away' appearance. The fine expanded lip, of carmine crimson, is clouded with a deeper tint round the orange throat.

L. × Claptonensis (L. elegans × L. Dormaniana).—Small, white with a rosy flush. The long shovel lip is brilliantly crimson, fading to a white edge.

L.-C. amanda.—A natural hybrid of which Catt. intermedia is one parent, L. Boothiana perhaps the other. Pale pink. The yellow throat and the bright rosy lip show lines of deep crimson, strongly 'feathered' on either side.

L. × Gravesiae (L. crispa superba × L. praestans).—Small, rosy white. The spade-like lip is magenta-crimson, wonderfully smooth and brilliant, with two little yellow 'eyes' in the throat.

L.-C. Tiresias (Catt. Bowringiana × L. elegans).—The petals are exactly oval, saving pretty twirls and twists at the edges—soft bright mauve, the narrow sepals paler. The funnel lip does not open wide, but in colour it is like the richest and silkiest crimson velvet, almost maroon at the throat; charmingly frilled and gauffered.

C. × Portia.—Parents doubtful, but evidently Catt. Bowringiana is one of them, Catt. labiata perhaps the other. Sepals and petals lively mauve, the latter darker. The funnel of the lip brightest rose, disc of the softest tenderest crimson imaginable, deepening against the pale yellowish throat.

L.-C. Tresederiana (Catt. Loddigesii × L. crispa superba).—Rather curious than beautiful. The narrow petals and narrower sepals are pallid violet; the labellum has a faintly yellow throat, and the dull purple disc of Catt. crispa; not evenly coloured but in strong lines.

C. × Mantinii nobilior (Catt. Bowringiana × Catt. aurea).—Raised by M. Mantin. Delicious is a proper word for it—neat and graceful in shape, rosy-crimson in colour. The lip opens widely, exquisitely veined with gold within. It has a golden tinge on either side the throat, and a margin of deeper crimson. The whole colouring is indescribably soft and tender.

C. × Mantinii inversa represents the same parentage transposed (Catt. aurea × Catt. Bowringiana).—Small like its mother, of brightest deepest rose. The lip, loosely open above, swells to a fine expanse below, of darker tint. Throat golden, charmingly scored with crimson-brown, like aurea. The disc shows an arch of dark crimson on a rosy ground. It will be seen that the influence of Bowringiana strongly predominates.

C. × Chloris (Catt. Bowringiana × Catt. maxima) much resembles the above. It is less brilliant, however; the lip does not open so freely, and the arch mentioned, though even darker, is not so effective on a less lively ground.

L.-C. Fire Queen.—Parentage not recorded. I have not seen this flower, nor even an account of it, but it received an Award of Merit, June 6, 1897.

L.-C. Lady Wigan (L. purpurata Russelliana × Catt. Mossiae aurea).—Dainty pink of sepal and petal. From the pale yellow throat issue a number of crimson rays which darken to violet purple in the disc.

C.-L. Parysatis (Catt. Bowringiana × L. pumila).—Rosy pink. The funnel-shaped lip opens handsomely, showing a disc of soft crimson with a white speck at the tip.

L.-C. Robin Measures is assumed to be a natural hybrid of Laelia xanthina × Catt. Regnieri, a variety of Catt. Schilleriana. Sepals and petals smooth dainty green, the latter just touched with a suspicion of purple at the tips. It has the shovel lip of Schilleriana, a yellow tube and golden throat, from which descends a line of darkest crimson. The ground-colour of the disc is white, but clouded with crimson-lake and closely barred with dark crimson up to the white edge.

L.-C. Bellairensis (Catt. Bowringiana × L. Goldiana).—So curiously like L. autumnalis that a close observer even would take it for that species. In shape, however, it is more graceful than the pink form, and in colour much more pale than atro-rubens.

L.-C. Tiresias superba (Catt. Bowringiana × L. elegans Turneri).—I heard some one exclaim 'What a study in colour!' It is indeed, and in form too—not large, but smoothly regular as pencil could draw. The sepals make an exact triangle, delicate rosy purple, netted over with soft lines. Petals broad and short, darker. Lip rather long, white in the throat with a faintest stain of yellow, the disc and edges of the lobes glorious crimson-purple, with a dark cloud above which stretches all up the throat. A gem of beauty indescribable.

C. × Browniae.—Bought as a hybrid of Catt. Bowringiana × Catt. Loddigesii, but it shows no trace of either parent. Very pretty and odd, however. The tiny little sepals are hardly seen, lost behind the huge pink petals. The lip also has pink lobes above a gamboge throat, and a bright crimson-purple disc.

L.-C. Albanensis.—A natural hybrid, doubtless the product of L. grandis × Catt. Warneri. Pale rosy-mauve, lip crimson, deepening as it expands, but fading again towards the margin. A large and grand flower.

L.-C. Aphrodite (Catt. Mendelii × L. purpurata).—Sepals and petals pure white. Labellum deepest crimson with rosy tip.

L. × Sanderae (L. xanthina × L. Dormaniana).—Sepals and petals crimson, lip purplish rose.

C. × Mariottiana (Catt. Eldorado × Catt. gigas).—Very pretty, dark rose, lip bright crimson with yellow throat.

L. × splendens (L. crispa × L. purpurata).—Pink. Lip crimson-purple, edged with white, heavily fringed.

C. × Atalanta (Catt. Leopoldii × Catt. Warcewiczii).—Large and waxy. Sepals and petals rose veined with crimson, lip bright magenta.

L.-C. excellens (Catt. gigas ocullata × L. purpurata Brysiana).—A superb flower, very large, rosy mauve, lip crimson.

L.-C. Amazon (Catt. maxima × L. purpurata).—Sepals and petals softly flushed, lip much darker in tone, veined with crimson.

C. × Prince of Wales (Catt. fimbriata × Catt. Wageneri).—White. The lip amethyst, veined with rose and frilled; throat golden.

C. × Kienastiana (Catt. Luddemanniana × Catt. aurea).—Sepals flushed white, petals warm lilac, the veins paler; magenta lip with shadings of orange and lilac towards the edge and a white margin.

L.-C. Hon. Mrs. Astor (Catt. Gaskelliana × L. xanthina).—Sepals clear yellow, petals white with a sulphur tinge; throat golden yellow veined with purple, disc rose, veined with crimson and edged with lilac.

L.-C. Broomfieldensis (Catt. aurea-chrysotoxa × L. pumila Dayana).—Mauve. The lip deep crimson, gracefully frilled; the throat has crimson and gold markings on a purple ground.

C. × Fowleri (Catt. Leopoldii × Catt. Hardyana).—Rosy lilac, lip crimson. The side lobes are white tipped with crimson.

C. × Miss Measures (Catt. speciosissima × Catt. velutina).—Pretty mauve-pink with darker lines. Golden throat, lip crimson veined with purple.

C. × William Murray (Catt. Mendelii × Catt. Lawrenceana).—Rosy with a purple tinge. Throat veined with orange and purple, lip purple-crimson.

L.-C. C.-G. Roebling (L. purpurata alba × Catt. Gaskelliana).—Sepals and petals flushed, lip deepest violet, suffused with crimson and edged with white.

L.-C. D. S. Brown (Catt. Trianae × L. elegans).—Soft pink, throat yellow with a brownish tinge, lip carmine-crimson.

L.-C. Mardellii fascinator (L. elegans Turneri × Catt. speciosissima).—Mauve. Throat yellow, darkening to orange in front, lip purple-crimson.

L.-C. callistoglossa (L. purpurata × Catt. gigas).—Sepals pale rosy mauve, petals darker. Throat yellow streaked with purple; lip purple.

L.-C. callistoglossa ignescens (Catt. gigas × L. purpurata).—Sepals rosy lilac, petals a deeper shade, lip glowing purple.

L. × Latona (L. purpurata × L. cinnabarina).—Pale orange. Lip whitish at the base, the disc crimson bordered with orange.

L.-C. Decia (L. Perrinii × Catt. aurea).—Pale violet, deepening towards the tips. Lip crimson, streaked with white on the side lobes, with white and rosy purple on the disc.

L.-C. Eudora (Catt. Mendelii × L. purpurata).—Rosy purple. Lip deepest crimson shaded with maroon.

L.-C. Eudora alba (L. purpurata alba × Catt. Mendelii).—Ivory white. Lip crimson with purple shadings.

L.-C. Hippolyta (Catt. Mossiae × L. cinnabarina).—Bright orange with a rosy purplish tinge. The lip red-purple, much frilled.

L.-C. Zephyra (Catt. Mendelii × L. xanthina).—All Nankin yellow except the crimson disc, which has a pale margin.

L.-C. Amesiana (L. crispa × Catt. maxima).—White washed with amethyst. Lip purple-crimson fading towards the margin.

L.-C. Exoniensis (Catt. Mossiae × L. crispa).—White flushed with rosy mauve. Lip purple-crimson.

L. × Yula (L. cinnabarina × L. purpurata).—Scarcely larger than cinnabarina, bright orange, the petals veined and flushed with crimson. The lip of size proportionate—that is, small—shows more of the purpurata influence in its bright crimson disc.

L. × Yula inversa (L. purpurata × L. cinnabarina).—The same parentage but transposed. More than twice as large as the other and spreading, but thin. Sepals of the liveliest orange, petals agreeably tinged with purple. On the long narrow lip this pink shade deepens almost to red. Upon the whole, neither of them is to be commended for its own sake, but the brilliant orange of cinnabarina is retained so perfectly that both will prove valuable for hybridising.

C. × Our Queen (Catt. Mendelii × unknown).—Sepals and petals white, faintly flushed. In the throat, of brightest yellow, are several brown lines. The upper part of the lip is crimson, the disc purple.

L.-C. Empress of India (L. purpurata Brysiana × Catt. Dowiana).—Sepals and petals rose, tinged with violet at the ends, lip large, spreading, of the richest crimson-purple.

L.-C. Leucoglossa (Catt. Loddigesii × L.-C. fausta).—Rose-pink. Lip white, touched with yellow in the throat.

L.-C. Henry Greenwood (L.-C. Schilleriana × Catt. Hardyana).— Sepals and petals cream-coloured, tinged with pink, the latter veined with rosy purple. Lip purple with yellow throat.

L.-C. Canhamiana (Catt. Mossiae × L. purpurata).—White tinged with mauve. Lip crimson-purple, with a narrow white margin, crisped.

L.-C. Pallas superba (L. crispa × Catt. aurea).—Dark rose. Lip purple in the throat, golden in the disc, finely striped with crimson.

C. × Wendlandiana (Catt. Bowringiana × Catt. gigas).—Bright soft rose, lip purple-crimson with two yellow 'eyes' beneath the tube.

C. × Cecilia (Catt. Lawrenceana × Catt. Trianae).—Sepals and petals deep violet, throat buff changing to violet, disc purple.

C. × Louis Chaton (Catt. Trianae × Catt. Lawrenceana—the same parentage as Cecilia but reversed).—A most successful combination. Fine in shape, petals soft rosy mauve, sepals paler, and superb crimson lip, with the yellow of Trianae strongly expressed in the throat.

C. O'Brieniana.—A natural hybrid of Catt. Loddigesii and Catt. Walkeriana apparently; pale mauve; lip yellow.

L.-C. Miss Lily Measures (L.-C. Arnoldiana × Gottoiana).—Very large. Sepals and petals dark rose; lip rosy purple.

L.-C. velutino-elegans (Catt. velutina × L. elegans).—Sepals and petals white with a yellow tinge, veined with rose. At the throat an orange blotch. Lip darkest crimson with white veins.

I append a list of hybrid seedlings which have not yet flowered and therefore have received no name as yet. It will be useful only to those who practise the fascinating art of Hybridisation. But such are a multitude already, and each year their numbers swell.

Cattleya labiata × Catt. Bowringiana.
" Mendelii × L. xanthina.
" Warnerii × L. Euterpe.
" Bowringiana × Catt. Hardyana.
" " × Sophronitis grandiflora.
" labiata × Catt. Brymeriana.
" Gaskelliana × Catt. Harrisoniae violacea.
" labiata × L. Perrinii.
" Bowringiana × L. Perrinii.
" granulosa × Catt. gigas Sanderae.
" amethystoglossa × Catt. Trianae Osmanii.
" labiata × L. Gravesiae.
" Bowringiana × Catt. Leopoldii.
" Schofieldiana × Catt. Schroderae.
" Schroderae × L. elegans.
" Harrisoniae × Catt. Hardyana.
" Bowringiana × L.-C. Clive.
" labiata × Catt. Brymeriana.
" Gaskelliana × Catt. Hardyana.
" Schroderae × L. grandis.
" granulosa × Catt. gigas.
" Gaskelliana × L. crispa.
" Mossiae × L. purpurata Schroderae.
" Leopoldii × L. crispa superba.
" Leopoldii × Catt. Harrisoniae violacea.

Laelia tenebrosa × Catt. gigas Sanderae.
" harpophylla × L. elegans Blenheimensis.
" cinnabarina × Catt. Skinnerii.
" tenebrosa × L.-C. Phoebe.
" "   Catt. Mossiae aurea.
" praestans × Catt. Lord Rothschild.
" Dayanum × Catt. labiata.
" cinnabarina × Catt. Trianae var. Mary Ames.
" purpurata × L. grandis.
" " × Catt. Schroderae.
" amanda × Catt. aurea.
" purpurata Schroderae × Catt. Mossiae aurea.
" Lucasiana × L. elegans Schilleriana.
" elegans × Catt. Mossiae.
" crispa × Catt. aurea.
" purpurata × Catt. Hardyana.
" " × Catt. Mossiae.
" tenebrosa × Catt. Warnerii.
" " × Catt. Mendelii.
" elegans × Catt. gigas.

Beyond the hybrids are twenty plants of white Cattleya intermedia. The owner of our collection was first among mortals, in Europe at least, to behold that marvel of chaste loveliness. Mr. Sander received a plant of intermedia from Brazil, which the collector labelled 'white.' Albino Cattleyas were few then, and Roezl alone perhaps ventured to imagine that every red species had a white sister. So they took little notice of the label at St. Albans. When Mr. Measures paid a visit, it was even shown to him as an example of the reckless statements forwarded by collectors. He, however, in a sporting mood, offered ten guineas, and Mr. Sander gladly accepted, but under a written proviso that he guaranteed nothing at all. And in due time Cattleya intermedia Parthenia appeared, to astonish and delight the universe. Several other albino forms have turned up since, all of which are represented here, but Parthenia remains the finest—snowy white, with a very long lip, which scarcely expands beyond the tube. That is to say, 'the books' describe it as snowy white. A careful observer will remark the faintest possible tinge of purple in the throat.

We have also a natural hybrid, Catt. Louryana, which the learned dubiously assign to intermedia alba × bicolor; all white saving the lip, which is mauve-pink with darker lines.

Among other albino rarities here is the charming L. praestans alba, pure as snow but for a plum-coloured edging round the upper portion of the lip.

L. Perrinii alba—stainless throughout. This exquisite variety also appeared for the first time in our collection.

L. Perrinii nivea—not less beautiful assuredly, though it has the imperfection, as an albino, of a pale pink labellum and a yellow throat.

Beyond these rise twenty-five stately plants of Angraecum sesquipedale, which we are learning to call Aeranthus sesquipedalis. There are those who do not value the marvel, though none but the blind surely can fail to admire it. In truth, like other giants, it does not readily lend itself to any useful purpose. I think I could design a wreath of Angraecum sesquipedale which would put jewelled coronets to shame; but for a bouquet or for the dress or for table decoration, it is equally unsuited. Wherefore the ladies give a glance of wonder at its ten-inch 'tail' and pass by, calling it, as I have heard with my own ears, a vegetable starfish. At Woodlands happily there are other flowers enough for a 'regiment of women,' as John Knox rudely put it, and they do not grudge the room which these noble plants occupy.

A LEGEND OF MADAGASCAR

I must not name the leading personage in this sad story. Though twenty-five years have gone by since he met his fate, there are still those who mourn for him. Could it be supposed that my report would come to the knowledge of two among them, old people dwelling modestly in a small French town, I should not publish it. For they have never heard the truth. Those kindly and thoughtful comrades of Alcide Lebœuf—so to name him—who transmitted the news of his death, described it as an accident. But the French Consul at Tamatave sent a brief statement privately to the late Mr. Cutter, of Great Russell Street, in whose employ Lebœuf was travelling, that he might warn any future collectors.

M. Leon Humblot has told how he and his brother once entertained six guests at Tamatave; within twelve months he alone survived. So deadly is that climate. Alcide Lebœuf was one of the six, but he perished by the hand of man. The poor fellow was half English by blood, and wholly English by education. His father, I believe, stuffed birds and sold 'curiosities' at a small shop in the East End. At an early age the boy took to 'collecting' as a business. He travelled for Mr. Cutter in various lands, seeking rare birds and insects, and he did his work well, though subject to fits of hard drinking from time to time.

At the shop in Great Russell Street, after a while, he made acquaintance with that admirable collector Crossley, whose stories of Madagascar fired his imagination. Mr. Cutter was loath to send out a man of such unsteady character. The perils of that awful climate were not so well understood, perhaps, twenty-five years ago, but enough was known to make an employer hesitate. Crossley had been shipwrecked on the coast, had lived years with the natives, learned their language, and learned also to adopt their habits while journeying among them. But Lebœuf would not be daunted. A giant in stature—over seven feet, they say—of strength proportionate, not inexperienced in wild travel but never conscious of ache or pain, he mocked at danger. When Crossley refused to take an untried man into the swamps of Madagascar, he vowed he would go alone. That is, indeed, the most fascinating of all lands to an enthusiast even now, when we are assured that the Epyornis, the mammoth of birds, is extinct. At that time there was no good reason to doubt the unanimous assertion of the natives that it still lived. Crossley was so confident that he neglected to buy eggs badly shattered, waiting for perfect specimens. His scruples were 'bad business' for Mr. Cutter,

65

as that gentleman lived to see, but they appeared judicious at the time. Fragments of Epyornis egg, slung on cords, were the vessels generally used in some parts for carrying water—are still perhaps. Besides this, endless marvels were reported, some of which have been secured in these days. Briefly, the young man was determined to go, and Mr. Cutter gave him a commission.

Thus Lebœuf made one of M. Humblot's guests at Tamatave. Another was Mr. Wilson, the only orchid collector there; for M. Humblot did not feel much interest in those plants, I believe, at the time. I have not been able to learn anything about Wilson's antecedents. His diary, upon which this narrative is framed, was lying about at Tamatave for years; we may conclude, perhaps, that the French Consul did not know to whom it should be forwarded— there was no English Consul. Probably Wilson travelled on his own account; certainly none of the great orchid merchants employed him. He was young and inexperienced; glad to attach himself, no doubt, to a big and self-confident old hand like Lebœuf.

Some weeks or months afterwards we find the pair at a large village called Malela, which lies at the foot of Ambohimiangavo, apparently a well-known mountain. Ellis mentions it, I observe, but only by name, as the richest iron district of the Central Provinces. They had had some trouble on the way. Among the hints and instructions which Crossley furnished, one in especial counselled Lebœuf to abstain from shooting in the neighbourhood of houses. Each tribe, he wrote, holds some living creature sacred—it may be a beast or a bird, a reptile, or even an insect. 'These must not be hurt within the territory of such tribe; the natives will readily inform you which they are. But, in addition, each village commonly has its sacred creature, and it will be highly dangerous to shoot until you have identified the object. As you do not speak the language you had very much better make it a rule not to shoot anything on cultivated ground.'

This was not a man to heed fantastic warnings, but he learned prudence before they had gone too far into the wilds. At a short distance from Tamatave, in a field of sugar-cane, Lebœuf saw a beautiful bird, new to him, which had a tuft of feathers on each side the beak—so Wilson described it. He followed and secured the prize. The semi-civilised natives with them paid no attention. But when, an hour later, surrounded by the people of the village, he took out his bird to skin, there was a sudden tumult. The women and children ran away screaming, the men rushed for their weapons. But collectors were not unfamiliar beings, if incomprehensible, so near the port. After some anxious moments, the headmen or priests consented to take a heavy fine, and drove them from the spot.

Their arrival at Malela had been announced, of course, and they found an uproarious welcome. All the people of the neighbourhood were assembling for a great feast. While their men built a hut of branches outside the fortifications—for no house was unoccupied—they sat beneath the trees in the central space. Such was the excitement that even white visitors scarcely commanded notice. Chief after chief arrived, sitting crosswise in an ornamented hammock—not lying—his folded arms resting on the bamboo by which it was suspended. A train of spearmen pressed behind him. They marched round the square, displaying their magnificence to the admiration of the crowd, and dismounted at the Prince's door—if that was his title—leaving their retainers outside. The mob of spearmen there numbered hundreds, the common folk thousands, arrayed in their glossiest and showiest lambas of silk or cotton. No small proportion of them were beating tom-toms; others played on the native flutes and fiddles; all shouted. The row was deafening. But doubtless it was a brilliant spectacle.

One part of the vast square, however, remained empty. Beneath a fine tree stood three posts firmly planted. They were nine or ten feet high, squared and polished, each branching at the top into four limbs; tree trunks, in fact, chosen for the regularity of their growth. In front was a very large stone, unworked, standing several feet above the ground. The travellers were familiar with these objects now. They recognised the curious idols of the country and their altar. On each side of the overshadowing tree barrels were ranged, one on tap, and another waiting its turn. This also they recognised. However savage the inland population, however ignorant of the white man's arts, all contrived even then to transport puncheons of rum through swamp and jungle for occasions like this. Now and again persons distinguished from the throng by costlier dress and ornaments were escorted to the spot and they drank with ceremonies. Wilson did not like the prospect. His companion had broken loose once before under a similar temptation. But there was no help.

Presently the Chamberlain, so to call him, approached with a number of officers, and invited them to attend the Prince. They found that potentate sitting at the end of a long file of chiefs. The floor of the hall was covered with snowy mats, which set off the beauty of their many-coloured robes. Beside the Prince squatted a pleasant-looking man in pink vest and white lamba. He wore a broad-brimmed hat of silky felt, black, with a band of gold lace, contrasting at every point with the showily-dressed chiefs around. This, they knew, must be the high priest, the Sikidy. The Prince received them courteously, but since their interpreter knew but little

67

French, and less, as it seems, of the language of this tribe, communication was limited to the forms of politeness. Then slaves brought in the feast, setting great iron dishes on the mats all along the row. Simultaneously the band struck up, and women began singing at the top of their voices.

The heat, the smell, the noise, the excitement of the scene were intoxicating without alcohol. But rum flowed literally in buckets, and palm wine several days old, which is even stronger. Wilson ventured to urge caution after a while, and at length Lebœuf tore himself away. Men came and went all the time, so their departure was unnoticed.

They reached the hut of boughs, now finished. Lebœuf threw himself down and slept; relieved of anxiety, Wilson set off to gather orchids. Malela appears to be a fine hunting-ground for collectors, but he only mentions the fact to explain his imprudence in leaving Lebœuf for some hours. The latter woke, found himself quite alone—for all the servants were merry-making, of course—and he also started off collecting. Unfortunately he traversed the village. And some of the chiefs took him in a friendly spirit to the barrel under the tree.

Wilson was returning—happy with a load of new orchids maybe—when he heard a shot, followed by a clamour of young voices. Next instant a swarm of children burst from the forest, and ran screaming across the open ground. Wilson had heard that cry before. His blood chilled. If the men of the other village were furious, how would it be with these drunken savages! He hurried to the spot whence the children had emerged.

As their voices died away he became conscious of shouting—an exultant tone. It was Lebœuf. They met in the outskirts of the wood. At sight of Wilson he bawled—

'Hi, young un! got any weeds to sell? Give you tuppence for the lot. Pretty flowers—all a-blowing and a-growing! Take 'em to the missus! The ladies loves you chaps. I say, what'll old Cutter look like when he sees that?' Lebœuf threw down an animal which he carried on his shoulder, and danced round it, shouting and laughing.

It was a small creature, brownish grey, with enormous ears very human in shape, long skeleton hands, and a bushy tail thicker than a lady's boa. By that and the ears Wilson recognised the Madagascar sloth, rarest of all animals then in museums, and very rare still. He had no particular reason to suspect that the natives reverenced it, but a beast so eerie in appearance and habits might well be thought sacred.

He implored Lebœuf to leave it and come away; Lebœuf did not even listen. After dancing and roaring till he was tired he picked up the aye-aye and marched on, talking loud.

Thus they did not hear the noise of a multitude approaching. But from the edge of the forest they saw it. Chiefs led the van, stumbling and staggering; among the foremost was that personage in snowy lamba and broad black hat—not pleasant-looking now. A mob of spearmen pressed behind. The clearing was a compact mass of natives, running, wailing, gesticulating—and they still streamed in thousands through the narrow gate. It was like the rush of ants when their nest is disturbed.

The sight paralysed even Lebœuf; Wilson, after an awful glance, ran back and hid. He could hear his comrade's shouts above the uproar for a moment—then there was a pause, and the interpreter's voice reached him faintly. Wilson still crept away. He heard only a confused clamour for some minutes, but then a burst of vengeful triumph made the forest ring. It needed no explanation. Lebœuf was overpowered. The noise grew fainter—they were dragging him away—and ceased.

For hours Wilson lay in an agony of fear. That Lebœuf was killed he did not doubt; but how could he himself escape, alone in the forest, ignorant of the roads, many weeks journey from the coast? A more cruel fate would probably be his. It might be hoped that Lebœuf's tortures had been short.

He did not dare push deeper into the wood; his single chance lay in creeping round the village after dark, and possibly rejoining his servants, if they still lived. If not, he might recover the road at least. But man could not be in more desperate straits.

Remaining thus in the vicinity, towards dusk he heard a whistle far off. The frenzy of his relief is not to be described—it was the rallying signal of the party. But suppose the enemy used this device to ensnare him? It might be! And yet—there was the hope. At worst they would give him a speedy death. He answered. Gradually the searchers drew near. They were his own men, led by the interpreter.

Wilson could not speak French, but he grasped that the natives would not harm him. Lebœuf?—It was almost a comfort that he could not understand precisely. The interpreter's pantomime suggested an awful fate. Lebœuf stood at bay with his gun, and the chiefs held him in parley while men crept through the brushwood. They threw a lasso from behind, and dragged him down. He was borne to the square, and after dread ceremonies which Wilson shuddered to comprehend, laid upon the altar.

In a maze of horror and anxiety he entered the village. It was not yet dark. But of all the multitude swarming there some hours before not a soul was visible. They had not left; every house

69

resounded with the hum of many voices—low, and, as it seemed to Wilson, praying. The square also was deserted; upon the high stone altar he saw a shapeless mass from which small wreaths of smoke still curled.

That was the fate of poor Lebœuf. The same night Wilson was seized by fever. He struggled on, but died within a few hours' march of Tamatave.

LAELIA PURPURATA

The next house is given up to L. purpurata with some L. grandis tenebrosa intermixed. Not much can be said of the latter species. Its extraordinary colour is best described as madder-brown, but here we have a variety of which the ends of the sepal and petal are yellowish. The broad lip, dull purple, has a madder-brown cloud at its throat, whence lines of the same hue proceed to the edges all round. The value of L. tenebrosa for hybridising needs no demonstration—it introduces a colour unique, of which not a trace can be found elsewhere. But as for the flower itself, I protest that it is downright ugly. This is à propos of nothing at all. Liberavi animam meam.

It is always difficult to realise that an orchid of the grand class is a weed. All our conventional notions of a flower revolt against the proposition. I have remarked that it seems specially absurd to an ingenuous friend, if one recall the fact while he contemplates Laelia purpurata. That majestic thing, so perfect in colour and shape, so delicately finished—a weed! So it is, nevertheless, as lightly regarded by Nature or by man in its native home as groundsel is by us. The Indians of Central America love their forest flowers passionately. So do those in the north of the Southern Continent. But I never heard that the Indians of Brazil showed a sign of such intelligence. The most glorious Cattleyas to them are what a primrose was to Peter Bell.

The obvious, unquestionable truth that Laelia purpurata is nothing but a weed has suggested some unorthodox thoughts, as I considered it, 'pottering about' my houses. This is not the place to set them down at length. But we have reached a less important part of the collection; I may chatter for a moment.

All things are grandest in the hot zone, from mountains to plagues. Excepting the Mississippi and the Yang-tse-Kiang, all the mightiest rivers even are there. We have no elephants, nor lions, nor anacondas; no tapong trees three hundred feet high, nor ceibas almost as tall; no butterflies ten inches across, no storms that lay a province waste and kill fifty thousand mortals. Further, all things that are most beautiful dwell within the Tropics—tigers, giraffes, palm-trees, fish, snakes, insects, flowers. Further still, the most intelligent of beasts are there—apes and monkeys.

It may well be doubted whether man, the animal, is an exception. In this very country of Brazil, Wallace found among the

Indians 'a development of the chest such as never exists, I believe, in the best-formed European.' No race of the Temperate Zone approaches the Kroomen in muscular force, and negroes generally are superior. The strength of the Borneo Dyaks I myself have noted with amazement. Black Papuans are giants, and the brown variety excel any white race in vigour. The exception is that most interesting Negrito strain, represented by a few thousands here and there from Ceylon to the Philippines. But even they, so small and wretched, have marvellous strength.

Thus all natural things rise to their highest level in the hot zones—I have to put the case very roughly, for this is a monstrous digression. Does it not seem to follow that man should rise to his highest level there? The aborigines are savages mostly and ever have been; no people of whom we have record has become civilised unless by an impulse from without, and none could reach the bulk of these. But India shows that the brain, as the form, of man may develop to perfection under the hottest sky. Therefore, to end this brief excursus, I conclude that as the tropical weed Laelia purpurata is more majestic and more beautiful than our weeds, so will tropic man some day rise to a height of majesty unattainable in our zone.

But the reader has had enough of it—and so have I; for to crowd a volume of facts and arguments into a paragraph is irritating labour. Let us get back to business. Here are some of our finest varieties of L. purpurata.

Marginata.—White of sepal and petal. It takes its name from the white margin surrounding the crimson purple lip. Very striking also is a large white triangle upon the disc, charmingly netted over with crimson.

Archduchess is faintly rosy. The lobes, closely folded, are deepest purple-crimson, over an orange throat. On either side the dark central line of the labellum is a pale blur.

Macfarlanei.—Sepals and petals very narrow, of a clear rose tint, with darker lines. A patch almost white in the front of the dark crimson lip.

Lowiana.—Petals rose, sepals paler. The tube is not large, but it, and also the labellum, could not be darker if still to be classed as crimson. Even the yellow of the throat is obscured, but there is a lighter blotch at the tip.

Tenebrosa.—The name is due apparently to branching lines of deep maroon which intersect the crimson lip. Petals and sepals are white, and there is a white patch on the labellum.

THE DENDROBIUM HOUSE

is the last in this series, where we see the usual varieties in perfection; there are pseudo-bulbs of Wardianum more than 4 feet long. At the present day, however, orchidists will not look at 'usual varieties' of Dendrobium with patience—nobile, cupreum, fimbriatum, thyrsiflorum, etc. etc. etc. They are exquisitely lovely, of course. Examine them as often as you will, new marvels of beauty appear. The fact is that most experts never do examine these common things; they look about for varieties. Such blasé souls can be accommodated, if needful. Here are specimens of nobile album, all white save the deep crimson blotch and a faint yellowish tinge upon the lip; nobile virginale, which has lost even this trace of colour; nobile murrhinianum, very rare, understood to be a hybrid with Wardianum, snow white, the tips of sepal, petal and lip purple, and a great purple blotch in the throat; nobile Cooksoni, no hybrid, but a sport, in which the ordinary colouring of the lip is repeated in the petals; nobile Ruckerianum, very large, the deep blotch on the lip bordered with white; nobile splendens grandiflorum, an enlarged and intensified form of the type.

Of hybrids I may name Leechianum (nobile × aureum), white, sepals, petals, and lip tipped with rosy purple, the great blotch on the disc crimson with a golden tinge. Ainsworthii, of the same parentage and very similar, but the blotch is wine-colour. Schneiderianum (Findleyanum × aureum), bearing white sepals, petals and lip tipped with rosy purple, throat orange, similarly striped.

Here are several 'specimens' of Epidendrum radicans, a tangle of fresh green roots and young shoots of green still more fresh and tender, pleasant to look upon even though not flowering; but verdant pillars set with tongues of flame at the right season. And an interesting hybrid of it, Epidendrum × radico-vitellinum (radicans × vitellinum),—brightest orange, the lip almost scarlet, with three yellow keels upon the disc; very pretty and effective.

Besides, we have here a Spathoglottis hybrid, aureo-Veillardii, Wigan's var. (Kimballiana × Veillardii),—most charming of all the charming family. Golden—the sepals tinged, and the petals thickly dotted with crimson; lip crimson and yellow.

STORY OF DENDROBIUM SCHRÖDERIANUM

Many who care nothing for our pleasant science recall the chatter and bustle which greeted the reappearance of Dendrobium Schröderianum in 1891. For they spread far beyond the 'horticultural circles.' Every newspaper in the realm gave some sort of a report, and a multitude of my confrères were summoned to spin out a column, from such stores of ingenuity as they could find, upon a plant which grew on human skulls and travelled under charge of tutelary idols. The scene at 'Protheroe's' was a renewal of the good old time when every season brought its noble plant, and every plant brought out its noble price—in short, a sensation.

The variety of Dendrobium phalaenopsis hereafter to bear Baron Schröder's name was sent to Kew by Forbes about 1857. This single plant remained a special trophy of the Royal Gardens for many years. It throve and multiplied. In course of time Sir Joseph Hooker was able to give a small piece, in exchange for other varieties, to Mr. Day, of Tottenham, to Baron Schröder, and to Messrs. Veitch. The latter sold their specimen to Baron Schröder; Mr. Day's collection was dispersed, and the same greatest of amateurs bought his fragment. Thus all three plants known to exist in private hands came into Baron Schröder's possession, and the variety took his name.

This state of things lasted ten years. Mr. Sander then resolved to wait no longer upon chance. He studied the route of Forbes's travels, consulted the authorities at Kew, and, with their aid, came to a conclusion. In 1890 my friend Mr. Micholitz went out to seek Dendrobium Schröderianum in its native wilds.

The man of sense who finds a treasure does not proclaim the spot till he has filled his pockets, nor even, if it may be, till he has cleared out the hoard. It is universally understood that Micholitz discovered the object of his quest in New Guinea. If that error encouraged the exploration of a most interesting island, as I hear, it has done a public service. And the explorers have not wasted their time. They did not fall in with Dendrobium Schröderianum, because it was not there; but they secured other valuable things. Very shortly now the true habitat will be declared. Meantime I must only say that it is one of the wildest of those many 'Summer Isles of Eden' which stud the Australasian Sea.

Micholitz arrived in a trading-vessel, the captain of which was trusted by the natives. Under that protection the chiefs allowed him to explore, agreeing to furnish men and canoes—for a consideration, naturally. Their power did not stretch beyond a few miles of coast; the neighbours on each side were unfriendly, or at least distrusted; and bitterly hostile tribes lay beyond—hostile, that is, to the people among whom Micholitz landed. All alike are head-hunters, and all charge one another with cannibalism—but falsely in every case, I understand.

The field was narrow, therefore, and uncommonly perilous, for the best-intentioned of these islanders cannot always resist the impulse to crown their trophies with a white man's head—as the Captain assured Micholitz day by day with an earnestness which became oppressive after a while. But he was very lucky—or rather the probabilities had been studied so thoughtfully before any step was taken that he sailed to the very island. I do not mean that it is wonderful to find an orchid on the first day's search when once its habitat is known. Dendrobiums cover a great tract of land. It is the nicety of calculation ten thousand miles away which should be admired.

There were no plants, however, just around the little port. After some days spent in making arrangements, Micholitz received an intimation that the chiefs were going to a feast and he might accompany them; there is no lack of interpreters on that coast, whence so many poor wretches are enticed to English or French colonies—some of whom return nowadays. The Captain could not go. In refusing he looked at Micholitz with a quizzical, hesitating air, as though inclined to make a revelation.

'Is there any danger?' Micholitz asked.

'Oh no! not a bit!—not a bit of danger! I answer for that. You'll be amused, I daresay. They're rum chaps.'

The chance of making a trip beyond the narrow friendly area in safety was welcome, and at daylight he started with the chiefs. It was but a few hours' paddling—to the next bay. The feast was given, as is usual, to celebrate the launch of a war-prau. In martial panoply the guests embarked, paint and feathers, spears and clubs. They were met by their hosts in the same guise upon the beach. After ceremonies probably—but I have no description—all squatted down in a circle, and a personage, assumed to be the priest, howled for a while. Then the warriors began to dance, two by two. It was very wearisome, and besides, very hot. Micholitz asked at length whether he might leave. The interpreter said there was no objection. He walked towards the forest, which stood some distance back, even as a wall, skirting the snowy beach. The grey huts of the village glimmered among palms and fruit-trees on one hand.

A sunken way had been dug from the edge of the surf to a long low building a hundred yards back; within it lay the prau doubtless, ready to be launched. Micholitz skirted this channel. He noticed a curious group of persons sitting apart—an old man, two women, a boy, and a girl. The elders were squatting motionless upon the sand, so bowed that the long wool drooping hid their faces; the children lay with their heads in the women's laps. None looked up; in passing he observed that these latter were bound.

The boat-house—so to call it—spanning the channel, was a hundred feet long, built of palm thatch, with substantial posts at due distance. As he walked along it, Micholitz became aware of an unpleasant smell. It was not strong. But in turning the further corner he marked a great purple stain upon the sand. Flies clustered thick there. It was blood. And then, upon the wall of thatch above, and the corner post, he traced the stain streaming broadly down. He looked to the other angle. The horrid mark was there also. They could not see him from the beach. Easily he parted the crackling palm leaves, and thrust in his head. At a few feet distance rose the lofty stern-post, carved and painted, with two broad shells glistening like eyes in the twilight. No more could he see, dazzled by the glare outside. That passed. He turned to the right hand-and drew back with a cry. A naked corpse, with head hanging on its chest, was bound to the corner post—the same to left.

Poor Micholitz felt sick. He ran from the cursed spot. So glowing was the sunlight round, so sweet and soft the shadow of the near forest—and those awful things in the midst! The old hymn rang in his ears—

> Where every prospect pleases
> And only man is vile.

He hurried towards the trees.

An outburst of yells and laughter made him turn. The circle had broken up. A swarm of warriors danced towards the boat-house— tore down the walls; in an instant the posts stood naked—with their burdens. Chiefs climbed aboard the prau and mustered, with tossing feathers, brandishing their arms, shouting and singing, on its deck. Ropes were manned. Scores of brawny savages started at a run, whilst the boys howled with delight and tumbled over one another. The great vessel moved, quickened. Then a party rushed upon that little group, trampling it under foot, snatched up the boy and girl, and sped with them towards the sea. The old man and women lay where they were tossed: there was no help for them in earth or heaven. The prau glided quicker and quicker amidst a roaring tumult. As it neared the sea, those small victims, tossed aloft from either side, fell across its course. Micholitz looked no more.

'Let me attend to my business, for God's sake!' he kept repeating.

But when he reached the trees his business was done. Those horrors had so disconcerted him that for an instant he saw long green stems of orchid perched upon the boughs without regarding them. But here was one from the top of which depended a cluster of rosy garlands, four or five, bearing a dozen, or twenty, or thirty great flowers, all open; and there a cluster snow-white—a crimson one beyond, darkening almost to purple. Dendrobium Schröderianum was rediscovered!

Of Mitcholitz's emotion it is enough to tell that it drove all else from his mind, or almost. When the interpreter summoned him he sat down and hobnobbed with those murderers and ate their dubious viands. The triumph was startling, so speedy and complete; but so much the heavier were his responsibilities. When, with a chilling shock, he recalled distinctly the dread spectacle, he said again:

'Let me attend to my business! I can't help it!'

All went well. So soon as the chiefs understood that this eccentric white man fancied their weeds, they joyously offered them—at a price. The time of year was excellent—early in the dry season. Next day Micholitz returned aboard and the Captain brought his ship round to the bay. But he would not listen to the story. 'I told you they was rum chaps, didn't I? Well, you see I told you true.' In three days, so plentiful was the supply, Micholitz had gathered as many as he thought judicious, and heaped them on deck. They could be dried while the vessel was waiting for cargo elsewhere, and he longed to get away from that ill-omened spot.

Still luck attended him. The Captain 'filled up' quickly, and sailed, as by agreement, for a Dutch port, where the orchids would be shipped for England. He arrived in the evening, the ship lay alongside the wharf; next day his precious cases would be transferred to the steamer. In great content Micholitz went to sleep; so did everybody else, the watch included. Towards morning the harbour police raised a cry of 'Fire!' It must have been smouldering for hours. Not a plant could poor Micholitz save!

On arrival, he had telegraphed his success, and joy reigned at St. Albans all day. Foresight and enterprise were justly rewarded for once. What a coup—what a sensation! Let us not speculate upon the language used when a second dispatch came in the morning.

'Ship burnt! What do?—Micholitz.'

The reply was emphatic: 'Go back—Sander.'

'Too late—rainy season.'

'Go back!'

And Micholitz went. His protest, had he insisted upon it, was unanswerable. Hard enough it would be to return among those anti-human wretches when the delights of home had been so near. But there was no chance of regaining the bay—a vessel might not sail thither for months or years. The work must be begun again—the search renewed. And in the rainy season, too!

But the good fellow did not even hesitate. Forthwith he inquired for a ship trading with the island. There was none, and he had no time to wait, for the rain grew heavier daily. A mail steamer was leaving for the nearest settlement. Trusting to the 'courtesy of nations,' Micholitz claimed a passage as a shipwrecked man. It was flatly refused, but at length the Dutch officials yielded to his indignant appeal so far as to make a deduction of 30 per cent. 'Well,' he wrote to St. Albans, 'there is no doubt these are the meanest people on earth.' The Captain of the Costa Rica whaling ship agrees with him.

I have no space for the adventures of this second journey now. The Dendrobe was found once more, which is not at all surprising when its habitat had been discovered. At this spot, however, it was growing, not on trees, but on rocks of limestone—most epiphytal orchids love to cling on that rough and porous surface. Especially was it abundant in the graveyard of the clan, a stony waste where for generations they had left their dead—not unmourned, perhaps— beneath the sky. The plants grew and flowered among bones innumerable. To suggest the removal of them under such circumstances was a nervous duty. But in the graveyard they were not only most plentiful, but by far most vigorous. It had to be done, and with all precautions, after displaying a sample of his 'trade,' looking-glasses and knives and beads, and so forth, Micholitz did it.

A clamour of indignation broke out. It was swelling into passion when he produced a roll of brass wire; at that spectacle it suddenly calmed down. After debate among themselves the warriors stipulated that two of their most sacred idols should travel with the plants, and be treated with all honour on the way. They would not assist in collecting, but after the distribution of brass wire they helped to pack the cases.

Thus it happened that one of the Dendrobes sold at 'Protheroe's' on October 16, 1891, was attached to a human skull. As for the idols, they were bought by the Hon. Walter Rothschild, and we are free to hope that they are treated with reverence, as per agreement.

STORY OF DENDROBIUM LOWII

The authorities assert that Dendrobium Lowii was introduced to Europe by Sir Hugh Low in 1861. My friend has so many titles to honour, in this and other forms of public service, that he will not feel the loss of one. The statement is not absolutely correct. An unnamed species, which must have been Dendrobium Lowii, flowered in the collection of Mr. H. Vicars, at Heath House, near Chelmsford, in 1845. I do not propose to describe the plant whereby hangs my tale; suffice it that this is a pale yellow Dendrobe, peculiarly charming, very delicate, and still rare. We do not hear of Mr. Vicars' specimen again. He obtained it, with others, from Fraser, Cumming, and Co., of Singapore, probably in 1842. It was brought to them from Borneo by Captain Baker, commanding the ship Orient Pioneer.

When lying at Singapore Captain Baker heard of the coal seams just discovered at Kiangi, on the Brunei river, which made such a stir in the City a few months afterwards. It seemed to him that his owners would like a report upon them. And he sailed thither.

I picture the man as big and rough—fat he was certainly; one of those sailors, careful enough aboard ship, who think it necessary to take a 'drop' at every halt when making holiday.

Pirates were no tradition in that era. They swarmed among the islands, and the younger chiefs were not proof against temptation when they fell in with an European ship that seemed to be in difficulties. Doubtless Captain Baker kept all his wits about him on a perilous voyage beyond the track of commerce then. But he reached the Bay of Brunei safely, ascended the river in a well-armed boat, and visited the coalfields at Kiangi. A few Chinamen were working there. Baker had shrewdness enough to see that immense capital would be required, that the Sultan would give endless trouble, and that the coal, when won, might prove to be dubious in quality. We may hope, therefore, that his owners kept out of the 'rush' which followed, and were duly grateful.

His business was finished. Messrs. Fraser and Cumming, indeed, had asked him to collect a few of the 'air-plants' which began to make such a stir in England, but that would not detain him. They grew so thick on every tree that a boatload could be gathered in dropping down the river. He had instructions to choose those upon the highest branches, where, as was thought, the best species are found; but it made no difference, for a sailor could walk up those trees hung with creepers as easily as up the shrouds! So

Captain Baker looked out for a place to land among the mangroves, expecting to fulfil his commission in an hour at most. A place was found presently, the boat turned to shore, and he directed a couple of sailors to climb. They were more than willing, under a promise of grog. I may venture to drop the abstract form of narrative here, and put the breath of life into it.

Baker had engaged a Malay as interpreter for the voyage; by good luck he was a native of Brunei. This man stared and laughed a little to himself on hearing the order. As the sailors began to mount, he said:

'Tuan Cap'n! Say 'm fellows looky sharp on snakes.'

The men paused suddenly, looking down, but Baker swore very loud and very often to the effect that he'd eat every snake within miles, and that Tuzzadeen was the son of a sea-cook. So the climbers went up, but gingerly. Tuzzadeen sat grinning. They had not mounted high, luckily, for on a sudden one gave a screech, and both crashed down, the second dropping in sheer fright. But he who uttered that yell had good cause for it, evidently. He danced and twisted, threw himself down and bounded to his feet, roaring with pain. His eyes showed the white in a circle all round, and his brows, strained upward, almost touched the hair. All leapt out, splashing through the shallow water, pale with alarm—seized their writhing comrade, and stripped him. Tuzzadeen examined his body; presently the convulsions grew fainter, and he struggled in a more intelligent sort of way, though still roaring.

'Him bit by fire-ant, I say, Tuan Cap'n,' observed Tuzzadeen.

'Well! Here's a blasphemous fuss about an unmentionable little ant! D'you call yourself a gore-stained British seaman, Forster? Just let's hear you do it, you unfit-for-repetition lubber, so as we may have a right-down blank laugh.'

Forster collected his wits and answered earnestly, 'It was an ant maybe. But I tell you, Cap'n Baker, there ain't no difference betwixt that ant and a red-hot iron devil. Oh law! I'll be good from this day. I know how the bad uns fare now.'

'That's a blessed resolution anyhow,' said Baker. 'But it didn't last above a minute, you see. Come, show yourself a man, and shin up them shrouds again.'

'No, Cap'n Baker,' he answered slowly and impressively, 'not if you was to put the Queen's crown on top of the tree and fix a keg of rum half-way up.'

Then they found that the other man had hurt himself badly in falling. Baker was stubborn. But promises and taunts failed to move one of them, and he was too fat to climb himself.

'Confound it, Tuz,' said he discontentedly, as they pulled into the stream. 'Other men have got these things. How did they do it?'

'Them get Dyaks—naked chaps what see ants and snakes.'

'Oh! And can I get Dyaks?'

'You pay, Tuan Cap'n, I find plenty naked chaps.'

In the evening all was settled. Tuzzadeen knew the chief of a Sibuyou Dyak village on a hill just above the bay; they would scarcely lose sight of the ship. No preparations were necessary. He himself would go ahead when they approached a village, and the Dyaks would be pleased to see them.

At dawn next day Baker started, with Tuzzadeen and four armed sailors. They crossed the broad white beach, studded with big rocks, moss-grown, weather-stained, clothed with creepers and plumed with fern; through a grove of cocoanut palms, scaring a band of children—Malay, but clad only in a heart-shaped badge of silver dangling at their waists—and entered the forest. There was a well-worn path. In a hilly district like this Dyaks are content to walk upon the ground; elsewhere they lay tree-trunks, end to end, on crossed posts, and trot along, raised above the level of the bush.

It is likely that this was the first time Captain Baker had entered a tropic forest. A very few steps from the busy go-downs of Singapore would have taken him into one peculiarly charming; but tigers lay in wait all round the town—so at least it was believed, not without probability. A few daring souls already dwelt at Tanglin; but they left business early, looked to their arms before setting out, and never dreamed of quitting the bungalow when safe home once more.

Anyhow, the good man was struck with the beauty of that jungle. Scarcely a flower did he see, or a butterfly, or any living thing save ants and wasps. Vast trees arching above the path shut out every sun-ray in that early hour. But all beneath them was a garden such as he had never conceived. The dews had not yet dried up. They outlined every thread in the great webs stretching from bush to bush, edged the feathers of bamboo with white, hung on the tip of every leaf. And the leaves were endless in variety. Like a green wall they stood on either hand—so closely were they pressed together along the track, which gave them some faint breath of air and glimmer of sunshine at noonday. Living things were heard, too, though unseen. The wah-wahs called 'jug-jug' in a long gurgling cadence, like water pouring from a bottle. Boughs clashed in sudden tumult, and dimly one caught a glimpse of monkeys flying through the air in alarm. A crow upon the top of some dead tree uttered its clanging call, slow and sonorous like strokes upon a bell. In short,

Baker was much pleased and interested. Often he came to a halt, and at every halt he served out rum.

It was a walk of some miles, very steep at the last. Near the village they crossed a ravine, dry at this season; so deep it was that the bridge which spanned it hung far above the tops of lofty trees growing on an island in the midst.

The bridge was actually the greatest wonder seen as yet on this delightful excursion. Huge bamboos, lashed end to end, were suspended over the abyss by rattans beyond counting, fixed in the trees at either side. Not only wonderful but most elegant it was, for the rattans had been disposed symmetrically. But Baker, though a seaman from his youth up, surveyed it with dismay. Boards a foot wide at the utmost had been laid across the bamboo. There was a hand-rail on each side, but so slight that he perceived it could not be meant for a support. Moreover, Tuzzadeen warned him earnestly, before leading the way, that he must not grasp the hand-rail—it must be touched only, to assist the balance.

Then the Malay went across. At a yard out the bridge began to shiver, and when he reached the middle, which dipped many feet, it was swinging to and fro like a pendulum. If Baker had not drunk just enough to make him reckless he would have turned back. A couple of the men refused. That was another prick of the spur. He followed Tuzzadeen, with his heart in his mouth, and arrived safely. Guess how deep was the refresher after that.

Tuzzadeen pushed on, and returned presently with an invitation from the chief—the Orang kaya, as his title goes. I can fancy Baker's astonishment when he came in sight of the village. It was one house, perhaps three hundred feet long, raised thirty feet in the air on posts. They climbed a notched log to the entrance, where the chief was waiting with his councillors. He had sent for young men, readily spared at this season, and meantime he asked the Tuan to rest.

Baker perceived that the house was open from end to end in front and on his left hand as he entered; on the right, however, stretched a wooden party wall, with many doors. He rightly concluded that the open space was common and each family occupied one chamber. Hundreds of people crowded round, especially children.

Then he lunched, the chief looking on, and in due time a score of stalwart young Dyaks arrived. After resting he started again with them.

What with drink and interest Baker was now jovially excited. In passing through the house he noticed a door festooned with greenery. A noise of howling came through it. He asked Tuzzadeen what this meant. Tuzzadeen, Malay and Moslem, was much amused.

'Baby born!' he laughed. 'Father go to bed; mother feed him with rice and salt.'

'Feed the father?' Baker cried.

'Yes. Them naked chaps say father's child, not mother's. Women cry over him. You hear?'

'Lord 'a mercy, I must see this!' And before Tuzzadeen could interfere he opened the door.

Wild uproar broke out on the instant, men shouted, women screamed and wailed—in a solid mass they rushed from the spot. Tuzzadeen caught Baker and ran him back up the passage, the sailors following. They fled for their lives, slid down the notched log and along the path, pursued by terrific clamour—but not by human beings apparently. Perceiving this, Tuzzadeen stopped.

'I go back,' he said breathlessly. 'Them kill us in jungle when them like. I make trade. You pay?'

'Anything—anything!' cried Baker. 'We haven't even our guns!'

So the Malay went back to negotiate, but they ran on—came to the awful bridge, Baker foremost. He reached the middle. One of the sailors behind would wait no longer—advanced and both fell headlong down. The sailor was killed instantly; Baker, in the middle of the bridge, dropped among the branches of a tree.

There he lay, bruised, half conscious, until Tuzzadeen's shouts roused him, and he answered faintly.

'Hold on!' cried the Malay. 'We come good time, Tuan Cap'n! Before dark!' Six hours to wait at least!

Baker began to stir—found he had no limbs broken, and thought of descending. His movements were quickened by the onslaught of innumerable ants, not a venomous species happily. But in climbing down he remarked that the tree-top was loaded with orchids, which he tore off and dropped; long before nightfall he met the search-party, toiling up the ravine from its opening on the shore.

Next day Tuzzadeen returned to bury the dead man and bring away the orchids; among them was Mr. Vicars' Dendrobium Lowii.

The Dyak practice referred to—of putting the father to bed when a child is born—prevails, or has prevailed, from China to Peru. It lingers even in Corsica and the Basque Provinces of Europe. Those who would know more may consult an Encyclopaedia, under the heading 'Couvade.' The house is 'taboo'—called 'pamali' in Borneo—for eight days. Hence the commotion.

CALANTHE HOUSE

For my own part I rank Calanthes among the most charming of flowers, and in the abstract most people agree with me perhaps. Yet they are contemned—the natural species—by all professed orchidists; and even hybrids mostly will be found in holes and corners, where no one is invited to pause and look at them. There are grand exceptions certainly. In Baron Schröder's wondrous collection, the hybrid Calanthes hold a most honourable place. I have seen them in bloom there filling a big house, more like flowering shrubs than orchids—a blaze and a mass of colour almost startling. But these are unique, raised with the utmost care from the largest and rarest and most brilliant varieties which money unlimited could discover. The species used for hybridising were, as I understand, Cal. vestita oculata gigantea with Cal. Regnieri, Sanderiana, and igneo-oculata—but picked examples, as has been said.

Here we have, among others, Sandhurstiana, offspring of Limatodes rosea × Cal. vest. rubro-oculata. The individual flowers are large, and a spike may bear as many as forty; brightest crimson, with a large yellow 'eye' upon the lip. No mortal contemns this.

Bella (Veitchii × Turneri).—Sepals white, petals daintily flushed; lip somewhat more deeply flushed, with a white patch upon the disc, and in this a broad spot of the deepest but liveliest crimson.

Veitchii of course; but also the pure white form of Veitchii, which is by no means a matter of course.

William Murray (vest. rubro-oculata × Williamsii).—A hybrid notably robust, which is always a recommendation. White sepals and petals, a crimson patch on the lip, darkest at the throat.

Florence (bella × Veitchii).—Flowers large, of a deep rose, with purplish rose markings.

Clive.—The parentage of this hybrid is lost. Petals lively carmine, sepals paler. Throat yellow, lip white at base with carmine disc.

Victoria Regina (Veitchii × rosea).—The large flowers are all tender rose, saving a touch of sulphurous yellow at base of the lip.

Phaio-calanthe Arnoldiae is a bi-generic hybrid (C. Regnieri × Phajus grandifolius).—Sepals and petals yellow; lip rose-pink.

Here also I may mention some interesting Phajus hybrids:—

Phoebe (Sanderianus × Humblotii).—Sepals and petals light fawn-colour with a pinkish tone; lip crimson, veined with yellow.

Owenianus (bicolor Oweniae × Humblotti).—Sepals and petals milk-white, tinged with purplish brown. Lip like crimson velvet, orange at the base.

Ashworthianus (Mannii × maculatus).—Sepals and petals deep yellow, touched with ochre, lip similarly coloured, marked with heavy radiating lines of chocolate.

Cooksoni (Wallichii × tuberculosus).—The sepals and petals are those of Wallichii—buff tinged with reddish purple, china-white at back; the lip is that of tuberculosus—side-lobes yellow, spotted with crimson; disc white, with purple spots.

Marthae (Blumei × tuberculosus).—Sepals and petals pale buff. The large lip white, touched with pale rose, and thickly covered with golden-brown spots.

Very notable is the Zygo-colax hybrid, Leopardinus (Zygopetalum maxillare × Colax jugosus), of which we give an illustration.

Here is also the Zygopetalum hybrid, Perrenoudii (intermedium × Guatieri).—Sepals and petals green, heavily blurred with brown. Lip violet, deepening to purple.

Against the back wall of this house stands a little grove of Thunias Bensoniae and Marshalliana; the former magenta and purple, and the latter white with yellow throat, profusely striped with orange red. The wondrous intricacy of design so notable in the colouring of orchids is nowhere more conspicuous than in Thunia Marshalliana.

THE CYMBIDIUM HOUSE

Our 'specimen' Cymbidiums, that is, the large plants, are scattered up and down in other houses; for singly they are ornaments, and together their great bulk and long leaves would occupy too much space. Here are only small examples, or small species, planted out upon a bed of tufa amidst ferns and moss and begonias, Cyrtodeira Chontalensis, and the pretty 'African violet,' St. Paulii ionantha.

Cymbidiums are not showy, as the term applies to Cattleyas and Dendrobes. Their colour, if not white, is brown or yellow, with red-brown markings. We hear indeed of wonders to be introduced some day—of a gigantic species, all golden, which dwells in secluded valleys of the Himalayas, and another, bright scarlet, in Madagascar. In fact, this was collected again and again by M. Humblot and shipped to Europe; but every piece died before arrival. At length M. Humblot carried some home himself, and a few survived. Sir Trevor Lawrence bought two, I believe, but they died before flowering. So did all the rest.

But if the Cymbidiums of our experience make no display of brilliant colour, assuredly they have other virtues. When eburneum thrusts up its rigid spikes, in winter or earliest spring, crowned with great ivory blooms, the air is loaded with their perfume. I have seen a plant of Lowianum with more than twenty garlands arching out from its thicket of leaves, each bearing fifteen to twenty-five three-inch flowers, yellow or greenish, with a heavy bar of copper-red across the lip. And they grow fast. It is said that at Alnwick the Duke of Northumberland has specimens of unknown age filling boxes four feet square; each must be a garden in itself when the flowers open. And they last three months when circumstances are favourable. Sometimes also—but too rarely—the greenish yellow of Lowianum is changed to bright soft green. Nobody then could say that the colouring is not attractive.

We have here most of the recognised species—Cymbidiums are not much given to 'sporting': Devonianum, buff, freckled with dull crimson—lip purplish, with a dark spot on either side; Sinensis, small, brown and yellow, scented; Hookeri, greenish, dotted and blotched with purple; Traceyanum, greenish, striped with red-brown, lip white, similarly dotted, and the famous Baron Schröder variety thereof, which arrived in the very first consignment, but never since; pendulum, dusky olive, lip whitish, reddish at the sides and tip; and so on.

The only hybrids of Cymbidium known to me are eburneo-Lowianum and its converse, Lowiano-eburneum. The former is creamy yellow, with the V-shaped blotch of its father on the lip; the latter pure white, with the same blotch more sharply defined—which is to say, that Lowiano-eburneum is much the better of the two. Both are represented here.

Against the glass, right and left all round, are Coelogynes of sorts.

We have another house devoted mainly to Cymbidium, in which they have been planted out for some years, with results worth noting. I am convinced that in a future day amateurs who put the well-being of their orchids above all else—above money in especial!—will discard pots entirely. Every species perhaps—every one that I have observed, at least—grows more strongly when placed in a niche, of size appropriate, on a block of tufa. There are objections, of course—quite fatal for those who have not abundance of labour at command; for the compost very quickly turns sour under such conditions if not watered with great care and judgment. Moreover, what suits the plant suits also the insects which feed upon it. And if there be rats in the neighbourhood they soon discover that there is snug lying against the pipes, behind the wall of stone. Anxious mothers find it the ideal spot for a nursery. I cannot learn, however, that they do any wanton damage, beyond nipping off a few old leaves to make their beds, which is no serious injury. I have rats in my own cool house. Many years ago, on their first arrival probably, an Odontoglossum bulb was eaten up. Doubtless that was an experiment which did not prove satisfactory, for it has never been repeated. However, rats and insects can be kept down, if not exterminated.

The Cymbidiums here were rough pieces, odds and ends, consigned to this house to live or die. Now they are grand plants, in the way to become 'specimens,' set among ferns and creepers on a lofty wall of tufa, the base of which is clothed with Tradescantia and Ficus repens. In front and on one side are banks of tufa planted with Masdevallias, Lycastes, Laelia harpophylla, and so forth.

STORY OF COELOGYNE SPECIOSA

Orchid stories lack one essential quality of romance. They have little of the 'female interest,' and nothing of love. The defect is beyond remedy, I fear—collectors are men of business. It is rumoured, indeed, that personages of vast weight in the City could tell romantic adventures of their own, if they would. So, perhaps, could my heroes. But neither do tell willingly. I have asked in vain. However, among my miscellaneous notes on Orchidology, it is recorded that 'W. C. Williams found Coelogyne speciosa up the Baram River. Books confine its habitat to Java and Sumatra.' The Baram is in Borneo. When travelling in that island thirty years ago I heard a story of Williams' doings, and I think I can recall the outline. But imagination furnishes the details, of course, aided by local knowledge.

It may be worth while to tell briefly how this gentleman came to be wandering in Borneo—in the Sultan's territory also—at a date when Rajah Brooke had but just begun to establish order in his own little province. Williams' position or business I never heard. Some Dutch firm sold or entrusted to him a stock of earthenware jars made in Holland, facsimiles of those precious objects cherished by the Dyaks. The speculation was much favoured in that day—it seemed such in easy cut to fortune. But they say that not a solitary Dyak was ever taken in. The failure was attributed, of course, to some minute divergence from the pattern. Manufacturers tried again, still more carefully. They sent jars to be copied in China, whence the originals came, evidently, at an unknown period. But it was no use; the Dyaks only looked somewhat more respectfully at these forgeries before rejecting them. For many years the attempt was made occasionally. Rich Chinamen tried their skill. But at length everybody got to understand, though no one is able to explain, that those savages possess some means of distinguishing a jar of their own from a copy absolutely identical in our eyes.

Mr. Williams had tried elsewhere without success, I fancy, before visiting Brunei, the capital. But he had good reason to feel confidence there. The Malay nobles would buy his jars without question, and compel their Dyak subjects to accept them at their own price; such was the established means of collecting subsidies. In fact, the nobles were overjoyed. But the Sultan heard what was afoot. He possesses several of these mystic objects, and he makes no inconsiderable portion of his revenue by selling water drawn from them to sprinkle over the crops, to take as medicine, and so forth.

For his are the finest and holiest of all—beyond price. One speaks upon occasion, giving him warning when grave troubles impend. Sir Spencer St. John says he asked the Sultan a few years afterwards 'whether he would take £2000 for it; he answered he did not think any offer in the world would tempt him.'

The Brunei monarch was shrewd enough to see that passing off false jars could not be to his interest. The Pangarans argued in vain. There's no telling where it would end, he said, if the idolaters once began to feel suspicious. 'Let your Englishman take his wares among the Kayan dogs. He may swindle them to his heart's content.' The Kayans were not only independent but ruthless and conquering foes of Brunei.

There was no other hope of selling the confounded jars. After assuring himself that the enterprise was not too hazardous, Williams sought a merchant familiar with the Kayan trade. He chose Nakodah Rahim, a sanctimonious and unprepossessing individual, but one whose riches made a guarantee of good faith. This man contracted to transport him and his goods to Langusan, the nearest town of the Kayans on the Baram, and to bring him back.

Williams was the first European perhaps to reach that secluded but charming settlement. The Nakodah prudently anchored in mid-stream and landed by himself to call on the head chief. When the news spread that a white man was aboard the craft, swarms of delighted Kayans tumbled pell-mell into their canoes and raced towards it, yelling, laughing, splashing one another in joyous excitement. But the great chief Tamawan put a stop to this unseemly demonstration. Rushing from the Council Hall, where he and his peers were giving audience to the Nakodah, he commanded the people to return, each to his own dwelling. Stentor had not a grander voice. It overpowered even that prodigious din. The mob obeyed. They swarmed back, and, landing, shinned up the forty-foot poles which are their stairs, like ants; reappearing a moment afterwards on the verandah, among the tree-tops. These vast 'houses,' containing perhaps a thousand inmates, lined each bank of the river, and every soul pressed to the front, mostly shouting—a wild but pleasant tumult.

The chiefs sent an assurance of hearty welcome. Williams paid his respects; they returned his call on board, and Tamawan invited him to a feast. Next day another potentate entertained him and then another. Drink of all sorts, including 'best French brandy,' flowed without intermission. Williams began to be ill. But there was no talk of business. His goods had been landed at the Council Hall, as is usual, but not unpacked. The Nakodah assured him all was right.

He himself had a quantity of merchandise waiting under the same conditions.

So a week passed; etiquette was satisfied, and Tamawan invited him to open his bales. The chiefs squatted in a semi-circle, all the population behind, in delicious expectancy. The jars were brought forth—first a Gusi, the costliest species, worth £300 to £1000 in 'produce,' among the Dyaks, had it only been genuine. This Williams presented, with an air, to Tamawan. The chief glanced at it, observed with Kayan frankness that for his own part he liked brighter colours, and, so to speak, called for the next article. Williams grasped the fatal truth when he saw how carelessly his precious Gusi was regarded, not by Tamawan alone but by all. Hoping against hope, however, he brought forth a Naga—a Rusa. The chiefs became impatient. 'Show your good trade, Tuan,' they said. Perhaps it was lucky that he had some miscellaneous 'notions'; but there was only enough to make the needful presents.

Utter collapse! The foolish fellow had not thought of asking whether Kayans valued these unlovely jars. Perhaps the Brunei nobles could not have told him, but Nakodah Rahim must have been perfectly well aware. By keeping silence he had transported a cargo of his own goods to Langusan at Williams' expense—without freight or charges! The victim could not quite restrain his anger, but it would have been madness to quarrel. He had indeed several Malays, perhaps trusty. But the crew outnumbered them, and the Kayans doubtless would back the Nakodah. There was nothing to be done but wait, with as much good temper as he could summon, until that worthy had sold out. During this time Williams hunted, explored the woods, and collected a variety of plants, some of which we do not recognise from the description. But among those he brought to Singapore was Coelogyne speciosa.

Meantime sickness attacked the crew, whilst Williams' servants escaped it. The Nakodah hurried his sales, but when he was ready to start, it became necessary to engage some of the latter, with their master's consent, for navigating the vessel; but for this mischance there would have been no need to ask the white man's co-operation in a little stroke of business.

At each of the festivities Williams had remarked a very pretty girl always in attendance on the chief Kum Palan. Charming faces are common among those people, and graceful figures a matter of course. Kayan maidens do not pull out their eyebrows, nor blacken their teeth, nor shave the top of the head, nor, in fact, practise any of the disfigurements which spoil Dyak beauty; for their tattooing, though elaborate, is all below the waist. Most of them even do not chew betel before marriage, and you hardly find one of these whose teeth are not a faultless row of pearls. Cool scrutiny reveals that their noses are too flat and their mouths unsymmetrical. But the girl would have a mane of lustrous hair decked with flowers, restrained by a snowy fillet over the brow, streaming loose down her back. Her skin would be pale golden bronze and her eyes worthy of the tenderest epithets. Even a chief's daughter wears little clothing beyond armlets and waist-belt of gold, white shell, and antique beads, as mysterious and as costly in proportion as the Dyak jars. Only a silken kerchief, clasping one thigh in studied folds, gathered and tucked in over the other, would represent what we call dress; but the tattooing from waist to knee is so close that feminine limbs seem to be enveloped in black tights.

Williams learned that this beauty was daughter to Kum Palan. Parent and child must be warmly attached, he thought, for she was always near him. Other chiefs had pretty daughters, but they received no such attention. The girl looked sad, but that is frequent with Kayan and Dyak maidens, when, in truth, their souls are dancing with fun and devilment—a mere expression of the features.

Nakodah Rahim's secret concerned this damsel—Kilian by name. She was in love with a youth, Nikput, popular and distinguished—he had taken heads already—but not yet in the position which Kum Palan's son-in-law ought to occupy. Other suitors did not come forward, however, for the eldest son of Tamawan, the Great Chief, entertained for the youth one of those romantic friendships common among warriors in Borneo. Tamawan could not interfere, but there was a general impression that he would not feel kindly towards the man who robbed Nikput of his bride. Kum Palan resented this state of things. He feared an elopement, and with good reason, for that was the little stroke of business which the Nakodah proposed. Nikput offered fair terms. All was arranged. On the morrow early the prau was to start, dropping down stream. It would anchor for the night, as usual, at a certain spot, and there the lovers would come on board, having taken such steps as should lead the pursuing parent in another direction. Nikput had a friend among the Milanaus lower down. When the disaster was beyond remedy, Tamawan would compel his subordinate to be reconciled. Would the Tuan object to this little speculation?

That the villain intended from the first to murder Nikput and kidnap his bride is certain. He declared at his trial that Williams had been his accomplice, and on this account Sir Spencer St. John held an inquiry. There was no shadow of evidence; the charge is grotesque. But it may possibly be that Williams exacted a share of the gold which Nikput agreed to pay.

All went well. At the time and place appointed, in pitch darkness, a canoe grated softly against the vessel's side—a few whispers passed—and Kilian climbed aboard. But, as it turned out, she was not wearing only a few ornaments and a kerchief. All the family jewels, so to speak, hung about her pretty figure. She was swathed in silk, garment over garment. And Nikput handed up several baskets that must have been a very heavy load even for his stalwart frame. They had looted the paternal treasure at the Nakodah's suggestion.

Next day passed without alarm; there are only farmhouses and villages, where a trader need not stop, between Langusan and the Brunei frontier. The fugitives remained below in the tiny cabin, amidst such heat and such surroundings that those who know may shudder to think of their situation. After dark, however, they came up, and, until he fell asleep, doubtless, Williams heard their murmuring and low happy laughter. On the morrow they would be safe.

A terrible cry awoke him—screams and trampling on the palm-leaf deck; then a great splash. Dawn was breaking, but the mists are so dense at that hour that the Malays call it white darkness. The sounds of struggle and the girl's wild shrieks directed him; but at the first movement he was borne backwards and overthrown by a press of men stumbling through the fog, with Kilian writhing and screaming in their midst. They tossed her down into the hold and threw themselves upon him, his own servants foremost. Perhaps these saved him from the fate of poor Nikput. What could he do?— he had no arms. They swore him to silence. But in that bloody realm of Brunei to whom should a wise man complain?

All that day and the next Kilian's shrieks never ceased. 'She will go mad,' Williams cried passionately; the Nakodah smiled. When her raving clamour was interrupted—died down to silence—they brought her on deck, a piteous spectacle. I have not to pain myself and my readers by imagining the contrast with the bright and lovely girl we saw a week ago.

They reached the capital, and Williams fled; of his after life I know only that he sold some orchids in Singapore. Happily the tale does not end here.

The crime would have passed unknown or unnoticed, like others innumerable of its sort in Brunei, had not Kilian avenged her own wrongs. She was raving mad for a while, but such a prize was worth nursing. Gradually she recovered her beauty and so much of her wits that the Nakodah sold her for a great sum to one of the richest nobles. A few days after, perhaps the same day, she stabbed this man and threw him from a window into the river—possibly with

92

some distracted recollection of her lover's fate. The Nakodah was seized and others. All the horrid story came out. They were executed, and the Sultan restored their victim—quite mad now—to her father. But on the way she leapt overboard.

CATTLEYA LABIATA HOUSE

This is the oldest of Cattleyas, for the plant now recognised as Catt. Loddigesii, which was introduced to Europe a few years earlier, passed under the name of Epidendrum. One might call labiata the 'eponymous hero' of its tribe, for Lindley christened it in honour of his friend Mr. Cattley, an enthusiastic amateur of Barnet. This was in 1818; from that year until 1889 Cattleya labiata was lost. It seemed easy enough to follow the journeyings of Swainson, who discovered it, and so reach the country where it dwelt; collectors innumerable made the attempt, but never succeeded. Mr. Sander, for instance, sent three at different times, expressly to trace Swainson's footsteps so far as they are recorded—Oversluys, Smith, and Bestwood; beside four others who skirmished along the track. He assured himself that they had explored every district which Swainson could possibly have visited; but of Cattleya labiata they found no sign. Meanwhile the plants of the first importation died off gradually, and the richest of mortals competed for the few surviving. Ten years ago, when the long search came to an end, very few were the persons in England who owned a specimen. I think I can name most of them—Baron Schröder, Sir Trevor Lawrence, Lord Rothschild, Duke of Marlborough, Lord Home, Lord Howe, Messrs. J. Chamberlain, Statter, R. H. Measures, R. I. Measures, Blandy, Hardy, Coleman, and Smith of the Isle of Wight. One of the examples possessed by Mr. R. H. Measures belonged to the variety Pescatorei, named after General Pescatore, the same leading amateur of early days whose memory is kept green by the sweetest of Odontoglossums, saving crispum. Cattleya labiata Pescatorei was a precious treasure then; 'none so poor as do it reverence' in this generation. The plant is still here, pretty enough so far as it goes, slightly distinguished by a silver edging to the petals.

The puzzle of that first consignment has not been explained—we have only eluded it, like Alexander at Gordium. Certainly Swainson did not find his plants in the neighbourhood where they exist at this time. It is conjectured that there were woods close to Rio, now cultivated ground, where it flourished at the beginning of the century. However, in 1889, Cattleya labiata reappeared; oddly enough a collector of insects found it originally, and a collector of insects rediscovered it. The 'professionals' were beaten to the last.

And now it has become almost the commonest of orchids; but for the same reason we may be sure that it will grow scarce again in no long time. Not to England only but to France, Belgium,

Germany, the United States, such vast quantities have been consigned that to one who knows something of the facts it seems amazing that the limited area could furnish so many. And for one that reaches the market three, perhaps six, die.

I have alluded to the extermination of orchids already. It is a sadly fascinating subject for those who think, and 'out of the fulness of the heart the mouth speaketh.' The time is very close when Odontoglossum crispum, most heavenly of created things, will arrive by tens and units instead of myriads—and then will arrive not at all. Already a gentleman who boasts that he has leased the whole district where the 'Pacho' form still survives, reckons the number of plants remaining at 60,000 only. Some months ago he issued quaint proposals for a Company (limited) to secure the utmost profit on the collection of these. Business men 'smiled and put the question by,' however enthusiastic they might be as orchidists; but I believe that the statement of facts was not altogether inaccurate. It is no longer worth while to send out collectors of Odontoglossum crispum; natives of the country gather such as they find and store them until the opportunity occurs to sell a dozen or so.

I could give other instances; some have been already mentioned. But what is the use? Unless governments interfere, there is no remedy. Some indeed have taken steps. Several years ago the Rajah of Sarawak decreed that no one should collect orchids in his territory, for sale, without a license. The exportation of Dendrobium Macarthiae from Ceylon is forbidden, and the authorities of Capetown have made stringent rules about gathering Disa grandiflora. But I have heard of no other restrictions, and these, commendable as they are, scarcely touch the mischief. But that is enough upon a melancholy subject, with which I have no need to meddle here.

In this house and elsewhere we have some eleven hundred labiatas. No Cattleya is more variable. From white to deep crimson every shade of colour may be found, with endless diversities of combination. Here are a few of the most important.

Imperatrix.—Rosy mauve. Distinguished by a broad fringe of the same colour round the lip, which, inside, shows a fine crimson. Next to it is one, unnamed, which makes a good contrast. Very big and broad; pale. The tube, opening wide, is superbly striped with crimson over a gold ground. The great lip all crimson.

Nobilis.—Big and evenly rosy. The gold in the throat is faint, and the lip, grandly frilled, has no lines.

Measuresiana.—Somewhat pale; at base of the petals the midrib is white. The gamboge stain does not spread beyond the throat, and it fades to white as the crimson lip spreads. Another has a deep golden throat, but the crimson of the lip is only a triangle, dispersing in broad lines upon the margin of mauve.

But here is one, on the contrary, in which the lip is all deepest crimson except a very narrow edging of white. Scarcely a trace of gold is seen; the crimson stretches back all up the throat in heavy lines.

And here again is one of palest rose, in which the lip carries only a single slender touch of crimson.

Sanderae.—A supreme beauty. Sepals almost white, petals somewhat more deeply tinged with mauve. Lip snow-white, saving the ochreous-orange throat and a lovely stain of crimson lake in the midst; with a purple blotch above and mottled lines of the same hue descending from it.

Mrs. R. H. Measures.—Purest white. The broad lower sepals curl downwards, almost encircling the lip, which has a faintly-yellow throat and a tender cloud of purplish crimson on the front, scored with three strong lines of purple.

Macfarlanei.—Crimson purple sepals and petals of the brightest tint; lip crimson-maroon and orange throat striped with brilliant crimson—a superb flower.

Baroness Schröder.—A famous variety. The petals are remarkably wide and graceful in shape, pale mauve of colour. The lip, somewhat paler, tinged with rose, shows in front a bundle of purple lines, as it were, the ends of which diverge from a purplish cloud over the rosy margin.

Princesse de Croix.—All pink except the white edges of the lip unrolling from the tube, and a small purple blur, scored with short heavy lines, which runs far up the throat, leaving a broad pink disc below.

Alba.—Perfectly beautiful. All ivory white, as it seems at a glance, save a faint stain of yellow in the throat; but close scrutiny detects a purple tinge also on the lip.

Archduchess.—The shape is even more graceful than usual. Sepals and very broad leaf-like petals rosy mauve, the yellow of the throat subdued, a fine patch of crimson lake on the labellum, with darker lines, leaving a wide margin of rosy mauve.

Robin Measures.—Rosy. The lip spreads so broad that its disc forms a perfect circle. The yellow of the throat is only a slight stain, and the fine crimson patch on the lip leaves a handsome margin of rose.

Bella.—Distinguished especially by the fine purple frilling of the lip which, like the sepals and petals, is nearly white of ground. A triangle of brightest crimson, sharply defined, issues from the handsome orange throat.

Adelina resembles this, but the crimson of the triangle has a deeper tone and the margin is distinctly mauve.

Princess of Wales.—An enormous flower, of remarkable colouring. Sepals and petals purplish. The usual crimson of the lip deepens almost to plum-colour. The margin, paler, is finely frilled.

Juno.—Somewhat pale. Notable for the breadth of crimson in the lip, which mounts far up the throat, running across it from side to side in a line perfectly straight.

Princess May.—A grand variety; the petals spread like birds' wings, and the lip opens very wide. On its folds are broad whitish discolorations, against which the deep crimson of the disc seems even richer than usual.

Her Majesty.—A pink giant, as notable for shape as for size. On the broad lip a crimson cloud stands out against a pale margin, finely frilled.

The edging of the central stand in this house should be noticed. It is formed by a single plant of Pothos aurea, which, starting from the end wall, has already encircled the structure twice. Now it is hurrying to make a third turn. Pothos is the neatest of climbers, pushing no side-shoots, growing very fast, and thrusting forth its large leaves at equal intervals. The variety aurea is touched with gold here and there, and to my mind it makes the ideal edging of a stand.

To right in this house is Cattleya Lawrenceana, of which we have probably 150 plants. This again is a species threatened with extinction—indeed the threat is very near fulfilment. It was never common in its native woods. I may quote a few lines from the report of Mr. Seyler who went to collect this, and two other orchids which dwell on the Roraima Mountain, for Mr. Sander; the date is January 19, 1893:—

'... I collected everything at Roraima except Catt. Lawrenceana, which was utterly rooted out already by other collectors.... We hunted all about for Catt. Lawrenceana and got only 1500 or so, it growing only here and there.... What I want to point out to you is that Catt. Lawrenceana is very rare in the interior now.... If you want to get any Lawrenceana you will have to send yourself, and, as I said to you, the results will be very doubtful.'

The variety Macfarlanei has rosy pink sepals; petals of club shape, bowed, crimson, deepening towards the tips. Labellum long, narrow, all crimson of the darkest shade.

Noteworthy is a plant which we may suppose a natural hybrid of L. purpurata with L. elegans, resembling the latter in size, comparatively small, as in its narrow sepals and petals flushed with rose. The lip is very bright and pretty, with large clear yellow throat,

97

ringed with white; the disc, of lively crimson, has a purple margin finely frilled, and a whitish purple patch in front.

Among miscellaneous examples here is a handsome specimen of Cymbidium Devonianum, and a very remarkable hybrid of Catt. Gaskelliana × Catt. Harrisoniae—Mary Measures; rather ghostly but pleasant to look upon. Its colour of sepal and petal is palest mauve, the tube prettily lined and mottled with pale yellow; labellum, gamboge-yellow in the throat, fading towards the edge, and a pale crimson tip.

A STORY OF BRASSAVOLA DIGBYANA

Brassavola Digbyana is a flower for all tastes—large, stately, beautiful, and supremely curious; I use the familiar name, though it should be Laelia Digbyana. Charming are the great sepals and petals, greenish white, around the snowy lip; but why, the thoughtful ask in vain, does that lip ravel out into a massive fringe, branched and interlacing, near an inch wide? The effect is lovely, but the purpose inscrutable. In Dendrobium Brymerianum we find a puzzle exactly similar. But it does not help us to understand. Countless are the species of Dendrobium, many those of Laelia; but in each case no other shows this peculiarity.

Brassavola Digbyana was first sent to Europe in 1845 by the Governor of British Honduras, who named it in honour of his kinsman, Lord Digby. Once only had the plant been received since that time, so far as I can learn, until last year. But the second cargo, in 1879, 'went a very long way.' Messrs. Stevens have rarely been so embarrassed with treasures. The history of that prodigious consignment is worth recording.

It was despatched by Messrs. Brown, Ponder, and Co., of Belize, who dealt in mahogany and logwood—do still, I hope. That trade appears to be rather interesting. The merchant keeps a gang of Caribs, who have been in the employment of the firm all their lives perhaps. They go out at the proper season to find and mark the trees; fell them presently and return whilst the timber is drying; or amuse themselves in the bush, hunting and gathering miscellaneous produce. Then they float the raft down to Belize.

These Caribs are more or less descended from the Indians of Jamaica. Early in the last century the British Government collected the survivors of that hapless race, and planted them out of harm's way in the Island of St. Vincent, uninhabited at the time. They did not thrive, however, and in 1796 the Government transported them once more to the Island of Roatan, in the Bay of Honduras.

But an extraordinary change had come over the poor creatures. We are to suppose that when landed at St. Vincent their type was mostly if not wholly Indian; when taken away it was to all appearance negro. Probably a slave ship had been wrecked there, and the blacks, escaping, killed all the male Indians, taking the women to wife; such is the theory, but there is no record. A transformation so sudden and complete in such brief time is striking evidence of the African vigour, for in hair, features, complexion, and build the Carib is a negro.

99

But not in character. He has virtues to which neither red man nor black lay claim—industry, honesty, truthfulness, staunch fidelity to his engagements and readiness to combine. The mahogany cutters have a Guild, which holds itself responsible for the failure of any member to execute work for which he has been paid; it cannot be called a Trade Union, because, so far as I learn, it has no other purpose—except jollification. In brief, the Carib of Honduras is one of the best fellows on earth in his way. He looks down on all about him, negro and Indian and 'poor white.' If a stranger suspect him of trickery, he thinks it defence enough to exclaim—'Um Carib man, sah!' And so it is, as a rule.

Messrs. Brown Ponder had lately taken on a new hand—let us call him Sam. This young fellow had been wandering up and down the coast some years, doing any honest work that turned up. Thus he had served in the boat's crew of M. Sécard, when that gentleman was collecting orchids in Guiana. The experience had taught him that flowers have value, and he returned from his first visit to the bush, after entering the firm's service, with the announcement of a marvel. We may fancy the report which negro imagination would draw of Brassavola Digbyana. The mysterious fringe did not puzzle Sam at all. It was long enough to serve the purpose of chevaux de frise, to keep off monkeys and birds! M. Sécard used to give him a dollar apiece for things not to be compared with it! In short, here was a fortune for the gathering—and what terms would Mr. Brown offer him?

Mr. Brown offered nothing at all. Residents in Honduras are curiously apathetic about orchids even now. I think it may be said that no collector has visited their country, which is the explanation perhaps. Moreover, Mr. Brown well knew the liveliness of the Carib imagination. Sam had met with only one or two belated flowers, which he displayed. But the shapeless little cluster of withered petals was no evidence of beauty—quite the reverse. Everybody cut his jokes upon it.

It might be supposed that a man would carry his wares to another market under such circumstances. But that is not the Carib way; it would be a breach of loyalty. Good-naturedly Sam told Mr. Brown that he was a fool, with an adjective for emphasis. They were all adjective fools, he assured them daily. But to treat with a rival could not enter his mind.

The gang had returned to the bush when young Mr. Ponder came back from Bluefields. His partner mentioned Sam's idea as a jest in conversation when several friends were present. One of them recalled how Governor Digby had sent some orchids to Europe ages ago, which sold for a mint of money. Others had heard something of

100

the legend. Ponder, young and enterprising, inclined to think the matter worth notice. He inquired among the oldest inhabitants, Carib and negro. Many recollected the Governor's speculation, and the orchid also, when pressed. It was as big as a bunch of bananas, blue—no, red—no, yellow; shaped just like a boat, or a bird, or a star, or a monkey climbing a tree, and so forth. But all agreed about the fringe, 'now you come to mention it.' Ponder saw they knew nothing beyond the mere fact. But he made up his mind to get some specimens next rainy season, and judge for himself whether a consignment would be likely to pay.

In due time the cutters appeared with their rafts of timber. It was not the moment to broach an unfamiliar subject. Calculations awfully intricate for those honest fellows had to be made intelligible to them once more, and then to be discussed, approved, explained again, and finally accepted or compromised. The Caribs passed all day in argument and in measuring the logs over and over; all night in working sums of arithmetic on fingers and toes. At length the amount due was computed amicably, as usual, and paid. But then, not without embarrassment, the whole gang, 'gave notice.'

When such an event occurs, under such circumstances, an employer knows the reason. His Caribs have found gold. There is nothing to be said beyond wishing them luck. But Mr. Ponder asked Sam to get him a few of his orchids next rains. Sam declined, somewhat roughly. Mr. Ponder laid the dispute before the Guild, so to call it, which pronounced that Sam must carry out his proposal before leaving the firm's service.

The dry season was well advanced by this time, and all flowers had withered. Nevertheless Sam jumped into a canoe, swearing, and started up the river with a couple of Indians. In three or four days he returned with a boat-load of orchids, sent them to the warehouse, and vanished. They proved to be a miscellaneous collection, all sorts and sizes; evidently the men had just gathered anything they came across.

Mr. Ponder grew angry. It was an impudent trick, a defiance of himself and the Guild, such as no true Carib would be guilty of. Foreign travel had demoralised Sam. Those honest fellows, his partners, would be not less indignant, if the shameful proceeding could be laid before them. But all had gone up the river—to their gold-field, of course—and no one knew where that might be. Mr. Ponder got more and more warm as he revolved the insult. Business was slack. He decided to follow, and sent out forthwith to engage a crew of Indians; gold-diggers do not mind the intrusion of Indians so much, for when these savages have obtained a very little dust, they withdraw to turn it into drink. And they never chatter.

101

Moreover he had to find the Caribs' camp, and they are sleuth-hounds.

The search was not so hopeless as it might seem. Carefully reviewing the circumstances, Mr. Ponder felt sure that his Caribs had discovered their placer whilst collecting the felled trees—not before; that is, in the rainy season. Men would not wander far into the bush at that time. Probably, therefore, the scene lay pretty close to one or other of the spots where they had found mahogany. Of those spots he had a minute description.

The reasoning proved to be quite correct, but luck interposed before it had been severely tested. On arrival at one of the stations to be explored—after a week or ten days' voyaging, as I imagine—he saw a canoe just pushing out from beneath the wooded bank with two of the missing Caribs therein, going to Belize on some errand. Their astonishment was loud, but not angry; they had no quarrel with Mr. Ponder. After a very little hesitation they consented to lead him to the camp, the Indians remaining in their boat.

It was not a long walk, nor uncomfortable. A broad path had been cut to the top of the ridge, for hauling down the trunks, and the rollers had smoothed it like a highway; but not so broad that the great trees on either hand failed to overshadow it. Mr. Ponder questioned his guides laughingly. Was it a real good placer, with nuggets in it?—how much had they pouched, and was the game likely to last? They grinned and patted their waist-scarves, which, as he now remarked, were round and plump as monster sausages.

'Oh, I know that trick,' laughed Mr. Ponder. 'You've filled them with maize-flour for your journey.'

They whooped and roared with triumph. 'Say, Mis'r George, you tell nobody—honour bright?-not nobody?' One of them turned down the edge of his scarf, with no small effort—for it was twisted very tightly and secured. Presently the contents glimmered into sight—little golden figures, mostly flat, carved or moulded, one to three inches long. 'Our placer all nuggets, Mis'r George!'

Any child in those seas would have understood. The Caribs had discovered not a washing nor a mine, but a burial-ground of the old Indians, called in those parts a 'huaco.' There are men who make it their sole business to look for such treasure-heaps. Since they bear, in general, no outward indication whatsoever at the present time, one would think that the hunt must be desperate; but these men, like other gamblers, have their 'system.' Possibly they have noted some rules which guided the antique people in their choice of a cemetery. And if they find one in a lifetime—provided they can keep the secret—that suffices.

Mostly, perhaps, huacos are discovered by accident. So it was in the memorable instance on Chiriqui lagoon, where many thousand people dug for months and many brought away a fortune—for them. And so it was here. The Caribs told their story gleefully. From the crest of the ridge the land sloped gently down towards a stream. When they reached this place to secure the timber, now dry, the rains were very heavy. But Sam and another, heaven-directed, roamed down the slope. A big tree had fallen, and among its roots Sam's lynx eyes marked a number of the little figures, washed clean, sparkling in the sun-rays. These good fellows have no secrets of the sort among themselves. They dug around, assured themselves that it was indubitably a huaco; then returned, like honest Caribs, to float the trunks down to Belize, and fulfil their contract, before attending to personal interests.

They had cleared a space and built a hut of boughs, a 'ramada.' There Mr. Ponder found them assembled, smoking and sleeping after the mid-day meal. Warned by the guide's cheery shout they welcomed Mis'r George heartily—all but Sam; unanimously they asked, however, what on earth he wanted there, so far from home? Mr. Ponder told his complaint.

The gang resolved itself into a sort of court-martial forthwith, the eldest seating himself upon a stump and the others grouping round. There was a moment's silence for thought; then the president, gravely:

'You, Carib Sam, what you say?'

'Say d—— sorry, sah! Mis'r Brown an' all the Mis'rs make fool of me! Then Mis'r George come—I never see Mis'r George before! He says go to bush an' pick orchid—a month contract!—a month! But I found gold here, an' I want pick it up—have no more say! d—— sorry!'

Mr. Ponder relented. 'Why didn't you explain at the time, Sam?—I'm quite satisfied, Caribs! Sam and I will shake hands and there's an end of it!'

But the others were not quite satisfied. The president sat shaking his head. 'When rains come,' said Sam to him anxiously, 'I get Mis'r George two canoe-loads, six canoe-loads of orchid, an' no mistake!'

'There, men! That's final! Let's shake hands round, and wash away all unpleasantness—here's the wash!—drink it up! Now will you show me your huaco?'

First they showed him the plunder—hundreds of those little images, mostly human, in the rudest style of art, but pure gold; a large proportion alligators, some probably meant for birds, not a few mere lumps. Mr. Ponder calculated rapidly that the whole might represent three thousand pounds for division among ten men. But the Caribs began to fear that their huaco would prove to be a very small one. The yield had been failing in all directions lately. They had prospected round, but hitherto without success. No bones, nor weapons, nor anything but a few jars of pottery had been found. Such is the rule—without exception, I believe—in burial-grounds of this class, without cairn or statues; in fact, it is a mere assumption to declare them burial-grounds at all. Men who dug at Chiriqui told me that nothing whatever besides gold was found in that great area. The statement is not quite exact, but it shows how little turned up.

The forebodings of the Caribs were sadly verified. Mr. Ponder started back in the afternoon and they followed within a week— 'made men' if they had wit enough to keep their booty, but not so rich as they had hoped.

Next rains Sam loyally performed his promise. And thus it happened that Messrs. Stevens were overwhelmed with Brassavola Digbyana once upon a time.

LYCASTES, SOBRALIAS, AND ANGOULOAS

Occupy different compartments in one house. The first will not detain us. All the species which orchidists, in a lordly way, term common are represented here—of course, by their best varieties. I can fancy the wonder and delight of a stranger entering when the Lycastes Skinneri alba and virginalis are in bloom, remembering my own emotion at the spectacle elsewhere. Not many of the genus appeal to the aesthetic, and Skinneri in especial lacks grace. But unsymmetrical form and abrupt rigidity of growth are forgotten when those great flowers, so pure, so divinely white, burst upon the eye. Charming also are the pale varieties of Skinneri, such as Lady Roberts, a dainty rose, the petals only just dark enough to show up the labellum almost white; and Phyllis of somewhat deeper rose. Its velvety lip has a crimson margin well displayed by a small white patch upon the disc.

Leucantha, dainty green with white petals, is charming; a pan of aromatica with fifty or sixty delicate golden blooms makes a pretty show. But these things do not call for special notice.

There are varieties, however, of course, as the famous Lycaste plana Measuresiana, coppery, shining, with pure white petals, crimson spotted, and small white lip; plana lassioglossa, olive green of sepal and petal, with a bright rusty stain at the base; lip white, with conspicuous white spots.

Fulvescens.—Large and spreading. Sepals and petals reddish orange, lip clear brightest orange, so lightly poised that it quivers at a breath. It has as many as forty flowers from one bulb sometimes.

Denningiana.—Very large. Sepals and petals whitish green, lip brown.

Mooreana.—An extraordinary variety of L. Locusta, which itself is extraordinary enough. Reichenbach described Locusta in his lively way: 'Green sepals, green petals, green lip, green callus, green ovary, green bract, green sheath, green peduncle, green bulbs, green leaves—just as green as a green grasshopper or the dress of some Viennese ladies.' Mooreana is larger, and the heavy fringe of the lip has a faint yellow shade.

SOBRALIAS

It may be granted that all classes of orchid are not equally beautiful, but to compare one with another in this point of view is futile. Each has its own charm which individual taste may prefer, and to set Cattleyas, for instance, above Odontoglots is only to demonstrate that for some persons size and brilliancy of hue are more attractive than grace and purity. But in any competition of the sort Sobralias must rank high. They are all large, they have every fascination which colour can give, and the delicate crumpling of the lip, characteristic of this genus alone, is one of Nature's subtlest devices. Gardeners also approve them, for they need less attention perhaps than any others, and they grow fast. The sagacious reader will begin to ask by this time what are the disadvantages to set against all these merits? There is only one, but for too many amateurs it is fatal—the glorious flowers last scarcely two days. Certainly a spike will carry four or five, or even six, which open one after another. But then all is over till next year. And the plants are big, occupying much room. Therefore Sobralias are not favoured by the wise, when space is limited.

All are American, growing among the rocks and in the scanty soil of mountain districts. One reads of species so tall that a man on horseback must raise his arm to pick the flowers. This may be an exaggeration, but we have Sobralia macrantha gigas here six feet high, and Hookerae even topping it. Upon the other hand, that marvel, Kienastiana, has a very modest stature. Nearly all the species known are here—it is not a large genus: Lindeni, Hookerae, Lowii, macrantha and macrantha alba, xantholeuca, and Kienastiana, which has its story.

Measuresiana is uncommon; white, an immense flower. The vast lip, circular, daintily crumpled, is palest pink, with a deep yellow throat, round which the pink darkens to pale crimson. Sanderae also is white, faintly tinged with yellow.

In these days, however, it is the hybrids which interest us, and there are two of surpassing merit.

Amesiana (xantholeuca × Wilsonii).—Palest rosy lilac, somewhat more rosy in the centre—the crumpled pink lip is as round and as big as a crown piece. The cavity of the throat, orange, changes to gamboge as it widens; encircling this is a stain of tawny crimson. Lip rose, shaded with reddish brown.

Veitchii (macrantha × xantholeuca).—White, with a pretty orange throat. Round the edges of the lip, deliciously frilled and crumpled, is a broad band of purplish pink.

Here and there in this house, as room can be made, stand many fine plants of Laelia elegans. Beyond is a second compartment devoted to Lycastes and Seleneped, the name granted, for distinction's sake, to Transatlantic forms of Cypripedium; in the gardener's point of view, however, there is no difference between them, and such of these plants as call for notice, in my very narrow space, are described among the Cypripeds.

One rarity, however, I must not overlook—Miltonia Binottii, assumed to be a natural hybrid of M. candida and M. Regnellii; sepals and petals creamy yellow, tinged with lilac at the base and barred with cinnamon brown; lip pale rosy purple.

ANGULOAS

Nature has thought fit to produce many clumsy plants, and the well-balanced mind raises no objection so long as they remain in their proper place. A pumpkin is not a thing of grace, but then nobody calls on us to admire it. There is little to choose between an Anguloa and a pumpkin in the way of beauty; yet a multitude of people, not less sane to all appearance than their neighbours, invite one to mark and linger over its charms. This always seems very strange to me. I remember a painting of Adam in Paradise, exhibited by an Academician famous in his day—less perhaps for talent than for the popular belief that he wrote certain wailing letters signed 'A British Matron,' which the Times published occasionally. Adam was sitting on a flowery bank. The good Academician had all the Asiatic realm of botany before him, wherein to choose blooms appropriate for Paradise; he spurned them all, crossed the Atlantic, surveyed the treasures of the New World, and from the lovely host selected—Anguloa Clowesii! Upon a bed of these Adam sat—of these alone; nothing else was worthy of a place beside them. Evidently Anguloas have a fascination. But my soul is blind to it. We have all the species here.

STORY OF SOBRALIA KIENASTIANA

There are startling flowers of divers sort. Some astonish by mere size, as Rafflesia Arnoldii, which is a yard across and weighs fifteen to twenty pounds, or Amorphophallus Titanum, eight feet high and fifteen inches thick. The stench of these is not less impressive than their bulk; an artist who insisted upon sketching the latter at Kew fainted over her work. But many of the giants are beautiful, as the Aristolochias, like a bag of silk cretonne with mouth of velvet, wherein a lady might stow her equipment for an informal dance—shoes, gloves, fan, handkerchief, scarf, and, if need be, a bouquet; Bomarias, the Peruvian wonder, trailing a scarlet tassel three feet long and thick in proportion. Others are surprising without qualification, like Nepenthes, which dangle a water jug at the tip of every leaf. But among orchids alone you see flowers of familiar shape and ordinary class, which startle you by the mere perfection of their beauty. One of these is Sobralia Kienastiana. My first sight of it at the Temple Show is not to be forgotten. I had been thrilling and raving over a specimen of Cattleya intermedia Parthenia, 'chaste as ice and pure as snow,' when, turning to Baron Schröder's exhibit, I beheld this glory of Nature. It has all the advantage of 'setting' denied to so many among the loveliest of its fellows. That divine Parthenia must be regarded alone. It has no charm of environment. But the Sobralia is a thicket, green and strong and pleasant to the eye, crowned with the flowers of Paradise, snow-white, several inches broad, but tender and dainty as the lily of the valley. Though open to the widest, and exquisitely frilled, their petals are crumpled; you might think fairies had been gauffering them and left the work incomplete, surprised by dawn. Baron Schröder and Mr. Wilson of Westbrook, Sheffield, had the only plants in England then; M. Kienast-Zolly, Consul at Zurich, the only plant known elsewhere—a piece cut off when he sold the bulk. That such a marvel had a legend I did not doubt. It is, in fact, an albino of the common Sobralia macrantha; in speaking of it, by the way, to scientific persons, or in referring to books, the word 'macrantha' must be introduced. The family is Central American, and examples reach this country especially from Mexico. A variety so rare and so charming would be found in some hardly known spot. But orchids do not live in the desert. It would be strange if Indians had not noticed such a wonder, and if they noticed, assuredly they would prize it. They would not allow the plant to be removed under ordinary conditions; if a price were accepted it would be very high, but more probably no sum would tempt them. Therefore did I conclude at sight that Sobralia Kienastiana had its legend. And I traced without difficulty the outline which I have filled up.

M. Kienast-Zolly dwelt many years at Orizaba in Mexico, where he collected orchids with enthusiasm for his own delight. An Indian servant gave zealous help, partly, doubtless, for love of the flowers, but partly also for love of the master whose 'bread he had eaten' from childhood—and still eats, I believe. This man, Pablo, ceaselessly inquired for rarities among his own people, made journeys, bargained, bought, and by times, they say—but stole is not the proper word to use when an object has no owner nor intrinsic value. Pablo had a younger brother, a priest, in the neighbourhood of Tehuacan. They had not met since his ordination, until, once on a time, M. Kienast-Zolly visited those parts, and Pablo took the opportunity to spend a day and night at the Indian village, Nidiri, where his brother was priest. This ecclesiastic was an earnest man. He found no satisfaction in compounding the heathen practices of his flock for money, as do his fellows. His legitimate dues sufficed him—I daresay they reached ten pounds a year. He found a melancholy diversion in writing plaintive memorials to the Bishop. Week by week the good man raised his moan. He could not see very deep. It did not occur to him that the Christian faith itself, as the Indians understand it, is but a form of heathendom. The doings of which he complained were acts of positive worship towards the old idols. He demanded an investigation, special magistrates; in brief, the re-establishment of the Inquisition. The Bishop had long ceased to acknowledge these dolorous reports; doubtless they contained nothing new to him.

Out of the fulness of his heart a man speaketh, and after discussing family affairs, the Cura broached his spiritual sorrows. Pablo had not been trained at a seminary, and religious questions did not interest him. As a townsman, also, he had picked up some liberal ideas, and when the brother talked of converting his flock from their evil ways by force, he observed that opinions are free in Mexico nowadays. Then the Cura grew warm. Opinions? Rising hurriedly, he produced horrid little figures of clay or wood, actual idols, found and confiscated, not without opposition. When Pablo did not seem much impressed by these things—not unfamiliar, probably—he hinted suspicions more awful. There was a spot somewhere in the hills, frequented at certain seasons by these wretches, where they performed sacrifice. Blood was shed, and the Cura had reason to think—he dropped his voice, and bent across the little table to whisper awfully in his brother's ear.

109

'Why,' said Pablo, 'if you can prove that, the Government will interfere fast enough. It's murder!'

'I am not quite certain. But give me authority to arrest the Cacique—the head-man of the village—and some others! They held one of their impious festivals only last week. I met them returning just after dawn, crowned with flowers, all the men intoxicated. Oh no, it wasn't a mere drinking bout. The Cacique and that vile Manuele—whom I believe to be the priest—carried nosegays of the accursed flower the demons give them. I know it! They used formerly—the sons of perdition!—to bring it to my church and offer it upon the holy altar. And I—Heaven pardon me!—rejoiced in its beauty. With prayers and thanksgivings I laid the Devil's Flower before the Blessed Mother. I did not know! It will not be counted against me for a sin, brother?' So he went on, bemoaning his unconscious offence.

Pablo woke up instantly. What did the Cacique do with his nosegay since he was not allowed to deposit it on the altar? What sort of flower was it? All this seemed trivial to the agitated Cura. With difficulty he was brought to the statement that it resembled the Flor de San Lorenzo, but snow-white. Then Pablo showed much concern. These shocking practices must be made to cease; but first they must have evidence. That mysterious spot on the hills? Did his brother know where it was? No, he had only pieced together hints and fragmentary observations. They suggested a certain neighbourhood. It had never occurred to him to look for it. If his conjectures were sound, the place was desert. Indians always choose a barren unpeopled site for their ancestral worship, as Pablo knew.

He considered. There was a certain risk, for the priests might dwell by their idols. But most even of these look upon their Christian rival with reverence. He asked his brother how he was regarded? Indignantly the latter confessed that all these wicked folk treated him with the utmost deference. He had denounced them again and again from the altar, threatened to excommunicate the whole community—but the Bishop promptly crushed that idea. They listened in respectful silence, and went their own way. Pablo came to a resolve. He proposed that they should start before daylight and search for the accursed place. The Cura was startled, but he assented with passionate zeal; of his stuff, unenterprising, unimaginative, with room for one idea only, martyrs are made. Martyrdom he half expected, and he was ready. Whilst Pablo snored in his hammock, the good man prayed all through the night.

It was still dark when they set forth, and before even Indians were stirring they had passed beyond the village confines; but the sun was high when they reached the hills. These are, in fact, a range

110

of low volcanoes, all extinct now; the most ancient overgrown with trees and brushwood, the most recent still bare. Towards this part the Cura led the way. They passed through blinding gorges where no green thing found sustenance. Cacti and yuccas and agaves, white with dust, clung to the naked tufa. So they went on, mounting always, encouraged from time to time by some faint trace of human passage, which their keen Indian eyes discerned. But from the crest nothing could be seen save gorges such as they had traversed, and long slopes of dazzling rock.

The quest began to look hopeless, but they persevered. And presently Pablo noted something on the ground, at a distance, beside a clump of Opuntia. It was a bunch of withered flowers. Approaching they saw a cleft in the ridge of tufa masked by that straggling cactus. They passed through—and the idols stood before them! The Cura fell on his knees.

It was a small plateau, as white and as naked as the rest. In the midst stood three cairns, each bearing large stone figures, painted red and blue and yellow. Before each cairn was an altar, built of unhewn stones topped by a slab.

The scene was impressive. Pablo recalled his prayers in looking on it. The white and glittering dust lay even as a floor around those heaps of stone. All was still, but the painted statues seemed to tremble and flicker in that awful heat. Tiny whirls of sand arose, and danced, and scattered, though never a breath of wind moved the burning air. The shadow of a vulture sailing passed slowly from side to side.

The Cura ended his prayer, leapt up and rushed—his old black gown streaming like wings. He grasped the foremost idol and pushed and pulled with all his might—he might as well have tried to overthrow the rock itself. Another and another he attempted; all in vain. He paused at length, mopping his drenched face, disheartened but still resolved. Then he took stones and battered the features.

Pablo was scarcely disappointed. So soon as they entered that barren tract, he knew that the Flor de San Lorenzo could not live there. Approaching he scrutinised the altars. Heaps of ashes and charred wood lay upon them, beneath leaves and fruits and flowers, unburnt but shrivelled and crackling in the sunshine. Carefully Pablo turned these over. On the largest slab were found bones and dry pools of blood.

I have not room to follow the story in detail. Next day they started for Orizaba, the priest carrying a passionate recital of these discoveries to the Bishop. What came of it I do not know. Pablo returned forthwith, in pressing haste, accompanied by two soldiers. With these he called on the Cacique and charged him with human

111

sacrifice. For a while the Indian could not speak; then he vehemently denied the accusation. The conference was long; in the end, Pablo admitted his innocence of the graver charge, but the acts of paganry could not be disputed. He agreed to say no more about them, however, on condition that the accursed flower should be surrendered and destroyed in his presence. By evening it was brought. But he changed his mind about destroying it just then. As has been said, this was the pride of M. Kienast-Zolly's collection for many years; then it passed, the half of it, to Baron Schröder, and a quarter to Mr. Wilson. Shortly afterwards Mr. Measures secured the latter fragment.

The description of the sacred place certainly does not apply to an Indian temple. The cairns were graves of ancient heroes doubtless, and the figures portrait-statues, such as I myself have seen in abundance to the southward. The Indians made this desert spot a temple perhaps, and treated the statues as idols, when their places of worship were destroyed.

THE CYPRIPEDIUM HOUSE

Perhaps our collection is most famed for its Cypripeds. During twenty years and more the owner has been securing remarkable hybrids and varieties—labouring on his own account also to produce them. But the pretty house which lodges these accumulated treasures is not more than 48 feet long and 17 wide. No room here for vulgar beauties; only the best and rarest can find admission. There are, to be precise, 980 plants upon the stages, 169 hanging from the roof. They are close packed certainly, but a glance at the vivid foliage satisfies even the uninitiated that they have space enough. Orchids generally are the most accommodating of plants— the best tempered and the strongest in constitution; and among orchids none equal the Cypripeds in both respects. It is pleasant to fancy that they feel gratitude for our protection. Darwin convinced himself that the whole family is doomed. In construction and anatomy it preserves 'the record of a former and more simple state of the great orchidaceous family,' now outgrown. Such survivals are profoundly interesting to us, but Nature does not regard them kindly. They betray her secrets. All the surrounding conditions have changed while the Cypriped clings to its antique model—at least, it has not changed in proportion. Few insects remain, apparently, adapted to fertilise it and it cannot fertilise itself. In the struggle for existence, therefore, it is terribly handicapped. Man comes to the rescue, and no class of orchid accepts his intervention so readily.

It is a pretty house, as I have said. Experienced gardeners have a deep distrust of pretty houses. Picturesque effect and good culture can seldom be reconciled; the conditions needed for the one are generally fatal to the other. But here we have a pleasing exception. All is green and fresh—no brickwork, nor shelves, nor pipes, nor 'tombstone' labels obtrude upon the view. The back wall is draped with ferns and creepers, orchids peeping through here and there. A broad stand down the middle, accommodating five rows of Cypripediums on either side, has all its substructures masked with tufa, which bears a mantle of green. The side stands, each accommodating seven rows of pots, are equally clothed in verdure, moss and fern. At the end, through a glass partition open in the centre, is a fountain, with similar stands all round it. And—an essential point, whereby we understand the glorious health of all these plants—there is not one which the gardener cannot see perfectly as he goes by, and reach without an effort, saving those overhead in the middle. No chance of thrips flourishing unsuspected in this house, nor of slugs following their horrid appetite from pot to pot unnoticed.

Since it is especially the number of rare 'garden mules' which have won us renown, I ought perhaps to say a word in passing upon the matter of hybridisation. But what can be said in a few lines? It is a theme for articles and books, even in the hands of a smattering amateur like myself. The public has no suspicion how far this novel manufacture has been carried already. There is a hint in the tiny volume compiled by Mr. R. H. Measures 'for private circulation,' showing the number of hybrids in the genus Cypripedium of which he could hear. It contains more than eleven hundred items. Of these we have upwards of eight hundred in our collection. But it must be remembered, in the first place, that there is no authoritative list as yet; each inquirer must get information as he can. In the second place, that the number increases daily. Such a list could be framed only by an international committee of botanists, for in France and Belgium orchid-growers are as enthusiastic as our own; whilst in Germany, Italy, Austria and the United States, if the workers be comparatively few they are very busy.

It has often been suggested that an Orchid Farm would pay handsomely, if established in some well-chosen district of the Tropics and intelligently conducted. A gentleman resident in Oviedo, Florida, Mr. Theodore S. Mead, has carried the notion into practice on a small scale with startling results. I quote from the Orchid Review, June 1896:—

'I have built a small platform in the top of a live oak, about 45 feet from the ground ... where I propose to try seeds of some thirty or forty different orchid crosses, including pods from Vanda coerulea and Cattleya citrina, which are thought difficult to manage under glass...'

In September 1897 we hear further:—

'The season has been a very trying one, and though my orchid-eyrie in the live oak-top promised great success in June, it was very difficult to keep the compost in good condition during the hot, muggy days of July. Still, out of thirty-two crosses planted on a space of peat, 16 inches long by 12 broad, I obtained plants having first leaf of twenty-two of them—mostly Cattleyas and Laelias;— though a good many died when it was necessary to transplant them, on account of mould and algae threatening to swamp the tiny plants. A single plant of Vanda coerulea × V. Amesiana appeared, and is now showing its third leaf. This year I have repeated the cross Bletia verecunda × Schomburgkia tibicinis and have several plants in their first leaf; and also one of Bletia verecunda crossed with our native Calopogon pulchellus...'

In March 1899:—'... My seed-planting was very successful after June in polypodium fibre (fresh fern mats) in my tree-top eyrie, and from July till October I averaged 500 little hybrids transplanted to pots every month; about one-fourth still survive.... I had an ancient moss-grown magnolia chopped down and cut into slabs, some thirty of which I planted with orchid-seed and kept sprayed. The slabs coming from near the ground scarcely germinated a seed, but those from 20 to 30 feet up yielded from 2 to 3 up to about 150. I also tried oak bark, but while the seeds started promptly they were more subject to disease;... when transplanted to pots nearly all died.

'Note.—These magnolia slabs were placed in a green-house, not in the "eyrie."'

It is hardly worth while to quote the list of seedlings obtained by Mr. Mead through crossing plants of the same genus. But here are some successes which, very few years ago, would have been declared flatly impossible—as impossible as a fertile union betwixt cat and dog.

Cattleya amethystoglossa × Epidendrum O'Brienianum; a few plants alive.

Cattleya amethystoglossa × Epid. radicans; two plants alive.

Schomburgkia undulata × Epid. radicans; several plants.

Cattleya Bowringiana × Epid. cochleatum; several plants.

Epidendrum nocturnum × Epid. osmanthum and Epid. cucullatum, pollen mixed; several plants.

Cattleya Bowringiana × Epid. osmanthum (Godseffianum); three plants.

Bletia verecunda × Schomburgkia tibicinis; several plants.

Bletia verecunda × Calopogon pulchellus; one or two plants.

Schomburgkia tibicinis × Laelia purpurata; one plant.

The discovery that fertile unions may be concerted between species, and even genera, differing in all visible respects, gives profound interest to the study of hybridisation in the scientific point of view. We have gone so far already that classifications which appeared to be unquestionable have been rudely upset. That Laelias and Cattleyas should combine is not surprising, even though one come from North Mexico and the other from South Brazil. But what shall we say when Epidendrums combine with both?—with Sophronitis, Zygopetalum!—nay, with Oncidium!!—with Dendrobium!!! Sobralia proves fertile with Cattleya; so does Sophronitis. Spathoglottis has been crossed with Bletia and with Phajus. Zygopetalum with Colax, with Oncidium, with Epidendrum, with Odontoglossum. Schomburgkia with Laelia and Bletia. Combinations even more astonishing are reported, but for those named there is responsible authority.

I cannot go into detail; these remarks are designed only to call attention to the subject. Not all the bigeneric hybrids mentioned have flowered; and at the present time we have learned enough to be aware that possibly one parent will be ignored by the offspring—that a seedling of Epidendrum crossed with Dendrobium, for example, will bloom a pure Epidendrum or a pure Dendrobium of the species used; which in itself is sufficiently strange. But seedlings have actually been produced in every case which I have named. It is one of the fixed rules in biology that the offspring of different species must be barren—otherwise the parents are not truly species—and that different genera will not breed at all. But in most instances which have been brought to the test as yet, hybrid orchids of different species prove fertile, and some bigeneric crosses yield a progeny at least. What follows? Evidently that the genera or the species are not really distinct—in the cases given. Must we admit, then, that a Dendrobium of the Himalayas (crystallinum) does not differ generically from an Epidendrum of Mexico (radicans)?

This is not the place to argue it out; nor, in truth, would there be much profit in arguing the question while the number of facts to be adduced is still so small that error is not improbable. I hope I have made it clear that the hybridisation of orchids is the most fascinating of botanic studies at this time; which is all I have in view.

But professional 'growers' are not likely to help the cause of science much—no blame to them either. They cannot afford to make experiments which demand a great deal of time, and increasing attention, for years, from the most highly-paid of their staff—too probably remaining a dead loss after no small portion of a lifetime has been spent in bringing the produce to flower. A man of business must make such crosses as are most likely to pay in the shortest time—easy species, big, highly coloured. Under the best conditions he must wait three to six years, perhaps ten, or even more. Evidently the most valuable hybridisations in a scientific point of view would be those least likely to succeed; all would be doubtful, all would require a long term of years, and most would not 'sell' in the end probably. Such work is for amateurs.

I can mention only a few of the Cypripediums here which seem most notable, and it will always remain dubious whether I have chosen the best examples.

Bellatulum eximium.—The dorsal is small, low and spreading, white, with carmine specks along the edges, large red-chocolate spots inside. Petals closely depressed, mottled with carmine here and there at the edges, and spotted like the dorsal. Lip insignificant—white with a few small dots.

Olivia (tonsum × concolor).—Dorsal white above, changing to pink; base greenish, slenderly feathered with carmine. Petals bowed, flushed with pink, pink lined, dotted with carmine. Slipper pink, deepening to carmine along the front, fading at the toe.

M. Finet (callosum superbum × Godefroyae).—White with a faint rosy blush. At the base of the dorsal is a greenish tinge, which reappears somewhat stronger on the petals. There are a few specks of crimson on the latter, and a few crimson markings at the top of the slipper.

Gertrude Hollington (ciliolare × bellatulum).—A flower of remarkable size. The dorsal is low but exceedingly broad; white, very strongly scored with crimson. Upon the scores stand spots of maroon, and a crimson splash follows the midrib. The great broad petals are white of ground, but obscured at the base by a cloud of crimson-maroon, save the edges. Crimson lines, carrying spots and specks of maroon, overrun the whole. Slipper purplish crimson.

Macropterum (Lowii × superbiens).—Dorsal green, darker below. Petals long, curving downwards, greenish at base, heavily spotted; the ends clouded with purple. Slipper large, tawny purple.

Bellatulum album.—The pure white variety of this striking species, so densely spotted in its normal form. It was discovered by Mr. R. Moore when Assistant-Commissioner of the Shan States in 1893. The dorsal is very low, spreading and depressed; the high-shouldered petals clasp the slipper close all round, in such manner that their ends hang below its tip. Grandly beautiful.

Baconis (chlorops × Schlimii).—Very small, rosy. Sepals scored with a brighter hue. They reverse half their length, showing the back of brilliant rose. Slipper carmine.

H. Ballantine (purpuratum × Fairieanum).—Dorsal rosy white, ribbed with dark crimson branching lines. Petals greenish, lined, dotted, and edged with coppery crimson. Slipper purple above, green below, handsomely lined with crimson.

Barbato-bellatulum.—Takes after the latter parent in shape, but all purple; the white-edged dorsal lined and the petals finely spotted with a darker tint.

Mrs. E. Cohen (callosum × niveum).—All pinkish white, suffused with crimson, lined with crimson and speckled with purple. Slipper carmine-purple.

Cardinale (Sedenii × Schlimii-albiflorum).—Takes its name from the carmine slipper. White in general colour; the petals have a rosy base and rosy tips.

Chrysocomes (caudatum Warcewiczii × conchiferum).—Dorsal greenish-yellow, edged with white. Its tip or crest is most extraordinary, hanging forward like a tongue between high jaws

117

curved and serrated. The ochreous-greenish petals have an edging of crimson and an outer edging of white, prettily frilled and gauffered. They twine and twist through a length of ten or twelve inches, showing the crimson reverse.

Claudii (Spicerianum × vernixium).—The dorsal is white above, with a strong purple midrib, and a purple flush towards the edge; the base is olive green. Petals olive green, shaded in a darker hue, and tipped with purple. The slipper purple above, green below.

Beeckmanii (Boxalli sup. × bellatulum).—The yellow-green dorsal is broadly margined in its upper part with white, and marked profusely with large crimson-brown spots. The petals are depressed, spreading like wings, of madder-purple hue, lined and spotted, the lower margin greenish. Slipper dark purple, with a greenish toe.

Bellatulum egregium.—Doubtless a natural hybrid. The depressed dorsal is pale green, spotted with pink in lines. Petals and slipper white above, pale greenish below, with large pink spots all over. A most remarkable variety.

Brownii (leucorrhodum × longifl. magnificum).—The dorsal takes a very singular form. Narrow and almost rectangular, it is sharply constricted towards the top, then widens out again like the ace of spades. The colour is white, touched with green and rose. Petals long, narrow, with an edging of carmine, and outer edging of white; as they reverse towards the tip the colour is all rose. Big broad slipper, rosy, prettily spotted with carmine on the white lining.

Antigone (Lawrenceanum × niveum).—The big dorsal sepal is pink with a white border. Strong branching ribs of crimson spring from a base of vivid green and form a network. The drooping petals show a deeper pink, with similar lines and maroon specks; as does the slipper.

H. Hannington (villosum × fascinator).—The great dorsal bears a purple mauve cloud within its broad white margin, changing to dusky green at the base and scored with branching lines of somewhat darker mauve. Petals and lip greenish ochre, frilled and shining, lined with brown in dots.

Hector (Leeanum var. × Sallierii var.)—Dorsal white with a greenish-blue centre, traversed by dull brown lines. Petals yellow at the base, set with a quantity of short, stiff black hairs; changing to ochreous dun, the upper half bearing a dusky brownish network. Lip of the same dusky hue.

Myra (Chamberlainianum × Haynaldianum).—Tall, graceful in form as in colouring. The long narrow dorsal is pale green, edged with white. At the base is a patch of dusky chocolate and spots of the same tone run upward in lines. The pale-green petals, narrow and

118

rectangular, bear a few large dun blotches outlined with chocolate; their tips reverse, showing a faint mauve tint.

Aphrodite superbum (niveum × Lawrenceanum).—The same parentage reversed; as usual the produce is quite dissimilar. Its colour is white, purple-tinged except the margin, overlaid with a crimson network of dots. Another example from the same seed-pod has a palest pink network instead of crimson, and tiny dots of maroon. It looks like the ghost of its sister.

Arnoldiae (bellatulum × superciliare).—Whitish, with bold spots of crimson-brown arranged in lines upon the dorsal. Slipper purple-lake above, greenish below.

Arnoldianum (superbiens × concolor).—Dusky shining yellow, tinged at the edges with crimson, spotted and lined with the same. A hybrid remarkable for its shyness to flower.

Cyanides (Swanianum × bellatulum).—A dusky flower, of green and purple tones. The greenish dorsal is clouded at base, lined and spotted, with purple. Petals the same, but the spotting is darker and more distinct. Slipper clear purple.

Callosum Sanderae.—A sport or natural hybrid of most singular beauty. I remember the delighted amazement which possessed me when Mr. Sander unlocked a door and showed this exquisite flower just opening—a treasure hidden from all but the trustiest friends until it could be displayed at the Temple Show in 1894. The great dorsal sepal is white above, tender green in two shades below, with strong green lines ascending from the base. The petals, much depressed, are bright green, lined with a darker hue and tipped with white. The slipper yellowish-green.

It may be mentioned that the owner of this collection declined to accept 1000 guineas for his stock of callosum Sanderae three years after buying the original plant.

Aylingii (niveum × ciliolare).—Small, white ground. The dorsal and petals alike are boldly striped with carmine-crimson. Slipper all white.

Conco-Curtisii.—The triangular dorsal is bright green in the centre, with a dark crimson cloud at the base and crimson lines. The broad depressed petals are dark crimson, fading towards the tips, similarly lined. Slipper green at the toe, crimson above.

Conco-callosum.—The dorsal, almost a diamond in shape, is crimson, with darker lines extending from a greenish base; petals greenish, margined, lined and spotted with crimson. Slipper crimson-purple above, green below.

Alfred (laevigatum × venustum).—Strong ribs of crimson-brown circle up from a green base over the white dorsal, which is pointed sharply. The drooping twisted petals are brightest green above, with a white margin, changing to tawny crimson as they reverse. The whole heavily spotted with crimson-brown. Slipper green, broadly netted over with a darker tint.

Calloso-niveum.—Where the parentage is shown in the name it need not be expressed at full length. A pale flower, dorsal and sepals greenish at base, faintly tinged and lined with pink, dotted carmine.

Amphion (Harrisianum × Lawrenceanum).—The grand dorsal sepal—greenish-yellow, dotted and ribbed with coppery brown—has a broad white margin. Petals narrow and bowed, greenish at base, changing to copper; a few heavy dots. The slipper coppery.

Cowleyanum (Curtisii × niveum).—Dorsal low and spreading, purplish and lined with purple; the edges white. Petals purple, very much darker at base and tips, with a white outline above, and tiny speckles of purple. Purple slipper.

Conco-Lawre (concolor × Lawrenceanum).—Dorsal large, suffused and lined with purple, edged white. Petals green at base, margined and lined with crimson, with a few dots of chocolate. Slipper purplish above, greenish below.

Curtisii (Woodlands variety) does not depart from the ordinary form in its scheme of colouring, but all the hues are intensified, and the enormous slipper, tinged with green at the edge, is deepest crimson-maroon.

I may interrupt the dry enumeration with a story.

STORY OF CYPRIPEDIUM CURTISII

My tales do not commonly bear a moral. If one they have it is apt to be such as grandmamma teaches—foresight, perseverance, the habit of observation. Those virtues need no finger-post. They are illustrated by the story of Cypripedium Curtisii, and rewarded there, as they should be always, by a notable instance of luck. I have not heard of any special circumstances attending the first discovery of this plant. It was found in Sumatra by Mr. Curtis, travelling for Messrs. Veitch, in 1882—a large green flower, margined and touched here and there with white, the pouch vinous purple. This brief and vague description may suffice for readers who take more interest in romance than in orchidology. Mr. Curtis did not tell the world at large where he found the treasure. It was his intention, doubtless, to work the mine himself. But after sending home the first fruits, he was offered the Directorship of the Botanic Gardens at Penang, and left Messrs. Veitch's service. He may well have hoped to revisit Sumatra one day, but the opportunity never came. Messrs. Veitch knew the secret, doubtless, and kept it faithfully; but they took no steps. And so, the first consignment being scanty, no more arriving, and the plant growing in favour, Cypripedium Curtisii rose to famine price.

The St. Albans firm took note of this. The home of the new Cypriped was admitted. Sumatra yields a profitable harvest always, even of familiar species, and besides, there is an excellent chance—vastly stronger fifteen years ago—of finding novelties. An intelligent man upon the spot should be able to trace the route of an earlier traveller. One of the St. Albans staff was disengaged. In short, Mr. Ericsson, a Swedish collector of great experience, was commissioned to seek Cypripedium Curtisii. He sailed in 1884. Nearly five years did Ericsson wander up and down the island—that is, in the Dutch territory. Working at leisure from Bencoolin northwards, he searched the range of mountains which bounds it on the east, and often descended the further slope—visiting peoples scarcely known, whom the Dutch had not yet invaded. They proved to be amiable enough. Many fine orchids did he send home, and the issue of the search was patiently awaited at St. Albans.

It did not seem more hopeful as years went by. Mr. Curtis's footsteps were traced easily enough here and there; but the Dutch frontier officials rarely speak any language but their own and the Malay, nor does their discourse generally turn upon orchids when they have a visitor. It was just as likely as not that Ericsson had

121

already traversed the district he sought, without identifying it. Cypripeds, as a rule, occupy a very narrow area, especially the fine species. They are a doomed race, belonging to the elder world, and slowly following its inhabitants to extinction. That fascinating theme I must not touch; readers interested may refer to Darwin. The point is that a collector may skirt a field of Cypripeds very closely without suspecting his good fortune.

But travel in Sumatra at that time was more limited than it had been—more than it is now. The Achinese still held out—for that matter, while I am writing, comes news of a skirmish wherein three officers and nineteen soldiers lost their lives. Ten years ago that stubborn and fearless people not only defended their own soil but also made forays into the Dutch territory. Desperate patriots allied themselves with the Battas, a cannibal race dwelling between their country and the province of Tapanuli; and hatred to the white man—or rather to the Dutch—carried the Achinese so far, though strict Moslems, that they tempted these savages to move by a promise of surrendering all captives—to be devoured. Thus the northern parts of Dutch Sumatra were very unsafe. When Ericsson desired to explore there he was refused permission. At Padang, the capital, however, in 1887, he made acquaintance with the Controleur—Magistrate, as we should say—of Lubu Sikeping, a district which lies along the Batta country. This gentleman spoke Swedish—an accomplishment grateful beyond expression to Ericsson, who had not heard his native tongue for years. Promptly they made friends.

The Controleur had been summoned to report upon the state of things in his Residency. He presented a long list of outrages and murders. Scores, if not hundreds, of peaceful subjects had been not only plundered and killed, but eaten, on Dutch soil, in the last few months. He represented that active measures must be taken forthwith. The Battas, inhabiting a high tableland beyond the mountains, crept through the defile, ravaged, burnt, massacred, and trooped back, carrying their prisoners away for leisurely consumption. Before news of the inroad reached the nearest outpost they were half-way home. Smaller parties lay in wait along the roads, stopping all communication. They had not yet ventured to assail a post, or even a large village, but the Achin desperadoes urged them to bolder feats, and they grew continually more aggressive. An expedition must be sent. It need not be large, for the cannibals are not fighting men. The Governor was persuaded. He ordered a small force to be equipped, and meantime the Controleur returned to his station.

It was a rare opportunity for Ericsson. He begged permission to accompany his new friend, who good-naturedly presented him to the Governor. An historian may be allowed to say that the hero of this narrative is fat, and there is no offence in supposing that the most exalted functionary has a sense of humour. His Excellency appears to have been tickled. The cannibals would rage with disappointment in beholding this succulent mortal—beyond their reach. He laughed and consented. I have no details of the expedition striking enough to be set down in a brief chronicle like this. It was a slow and toilsome march through jungle and mountain passes, the Barizan range, where a score of determined men might have stopped an army. The Achinese proved that; they held the force at bay for hours in a gorge, though less than a score. But the Battas would not fight even when their capital was reached, on Lake Toba. The Rajahs submitted, paid an indemnity, gave hostages, yielded up the surviving victims, and undertook to have no more dealings with the Achinese. So the matter ended. Ericsson found some new plants in their country, and many old well worth collecting. Doubtless the results would have been far more important could he have wandered freely. But those demons of Achin hung upon the line of march, joyously sacrificing their own lives to kill a Dutchman. If his personal adventures were not so curious, however—perhaps I should rather say so dramatic—that I could single out one of them, Ericsson gained much information about an extraordinary people. I can only set down a few facts.

He says that the Battas themselves do not regard their cannibalism as an immemorial practice. They have a story, not worth repeating, to account for it. But I may observe that if Marco Polo's 'kingdom of Mangi, called Concha,' lay in those parts, as geographers believe, some race of the neighbourhood was cannibal in the thirteenth century. 'They commonly eat men's flesh, if the person die not of sickness, as better tasted than others.' That is the motive still—the only one adduced—mere liking. Elsewhere the practice may be due to superstition in one form or another; among the Battas it is simply gourmandise. The head Rajah questioned gave a matter-of-fact answer. 'You Dutch eat pig,' said he, 'because you like it; we eat man because that is our fancy.' To be devoured alive is the punishment of four offences among themselves— adultery, robbery after nightfall, unprovoked assault, and marrying within the clan; the last an interesting item of which Sir John Lubbock should certainly take note for his next edition of The Origin of Civilisation. The instinct of 'exogamy' has no such striking illustration elsewhere. As for foreigners and strangers there is no rule; they are devoured at sight. And it may well be believed that people so fond of eating one another do not demand unquestionable evidence when a man of low station is charged with one of the four crimes which may give them a meal. I must not repeat the horrors which Ericsson learned. Suffice it that the victim is tied up, and those present exercise their choice of morsels. At a former time, they say, not long ago, the flesh was cooked—a statement which confirms the theory, so far as it goes, of a recent introduction. At this present they dip the slice in salt and pepper and eat it on the spot.

A good many missionaries, English, Dutch, French, and American, have not only settled on the confines of the Batta territory, but have travelled in the interior. The earliest of these, Messrs. Ward and Burton, found the people kindly, which again must be noted as suggesting that they were not so ferocious in 1820. The second party, Messrs. Lyman and Munson, of Massachusetts, were eaten. Mdme. Pfeiffer nearly crossed the tableland unmolested, though the savages were not friendly; but, as she says, they regarded her as a witch. Encouraged by this example, three French priests made an attempt two years later; they were promptly devoured. Two Dutchmen shared their fate not long afterwards, and the Government forbade more experiments.

I have no room for detail, but one very curious point must be indicated. These cannibals unredeemed possess an alphabet of their own, bearing no resemblance to the Malay, which latter is a corrupt amalgamation of Arabian, Persian, and Tamil. The Batta characters are original. They write commonly on strips of bamboo, scratching the letters.

On the return of the expedition, a party of invalids was despatched to the local sanitarium on Selimbang Hill, and Ericsson obtained leave to accompany it. There was no danger now. A few huts had been built there for troops, and a bungalow for officers— who made him welcome, of course. They arrived at dusk. The officers went out early next morning to their duties, and Ericsson lay waiting for his coffee. The rough timbers of the bungalow were concealed by boards, smooth and neat. Invalids quartered there had amused themselves by scribbling their names. Some, more ambitious, added verses, epigrams, and caricatures; others, drawings and even paintings. From his bed-place Ericsson scrutinised these artless memorials in the early light. Presently he observed a flower—a Cypripedium; the shape could not be mistaken. It was coloured, but dimly—the tints had soaked into the wood. With professional interest his eye lingered on this sketch. And then the first sun-ray streamed across the verandah and fell upon the very spot. Its faded colours shone brightly for a moment, green, white margin, vinous purple—Ericsson sprang out of bed.

No room for doubt! To make assurance doubly sure there was an inscription—'C. C.'s contribution to the adornment of this room.'

Hurriedly he sought a pencil and wrote—'Contribution accepted. Cypripedium collected, C. E.'

It was not such a smart réplique as the occasion seems to demand. But Ericsson is perfectly well satisfied with it to this day.

We can imagine how blithely he set to work that morning. Cypripedium Curtisii was selling in London at the moment for many guineas—a small plant too. And he had found the goose with golden eggs innumerable, waiting to be picked up. These orchids 'travel' well. There was no great distance to carry them before embarkation. The good fellow's fortune was made, and he had the pleasure of knowing it well earned.

With such cheerful thoughts, Ericsson sallied out day after day for a while, searching the mountain. He had a following of miscellaneous 'natives' by this time, experienced in their work. The neighbourhood was rich. Every evening they brought in a load of orchids more or less valuable, but never Cypripedium Curtisii. He engaged men of the district and showed them the picture. Some recognised it, and undertook to bring specimens; but they were always mistaken. The invalids withdrew, one after another. Ericsson found himself alone. His accumulated spoil of plants, well worth shipping, began to be as much as he could transport. As time went by, despair possessed him. After all, it did not follow that Mr. Curtis had found the prize just here because he painted it on the wall. To discover a new and fine orchid is a great achievement, and the lucky man might very well commemorate it anywhere when choosing a device.

Finally, 'time was up.' To wait longer would be sacrificing the great heap of treasures secured. After shipping them he might return. It was a sad disappointment after such reasonable hopes, but things might have been worse. So Ericsson gave orders to pack and start as soon as possible. When all was ready, on the very evening before departure, one of the local assistants brought him a flower. This time it was right. In three days several thousand plants had been collected, and Ericsson went his way rejoicing.

No reader, I hope, will fancy that these coincidences are invented. The story would be childish as fiction. It is literal fact, and therefore only is it worth telling.

William Lloyd (bellatulum × Swanianum).—The white crest of the dorsal rises from a dull crimson blur with greenish centre, overrun with crimson lines. The petals have a dull crimson ground, paler below, densely speckled with maroon, the ends just tipped with white. Slipper, shining maroon.

A de Lairesse (Curtisii × Rothschildianum).—The fine dorsal is white, with a greenish centre and faint purple edges, the lines clear purple. Petals long and drooping, pale green, edged with white; all covered with purple spots. Slipper, ochreous brown.

Juno (Fairieanum × callosum).—The broad white dorsal, green at base, tinged with purple, and strongly scored with purple lines, is actually the widest part of the flower, as in Fairieanum. The narrow petals curl down close upon the slipper, green in paler and darker shades, with bunches of purple hair, like those on a caterpillar, at the edges, and pale purple tips. Slipper, dusky greenish with brown lines.

Saide Lloyd (venustum × Godefroyae).—Dorsal small, bright green with darker lines. Petals purplish above, greenish below, speckled with small dots of crimson and strong spots of maroon. Slipper, ochreous yellow, dotted with crimson at top and netted with green.

Cymatodes (Curtisii × Veitchii).—The fine dorsal is green, fading to white, with a pretty narrow edging of pink, and boldly ribbed. The petals, dark at base, change to green, and towards the tips have an edging of profuse crimson specks. The slipper, very wide at the mouth, is greenish.

Dauthierii albino.—A wonderful sport. Up the grass-green dorsal, edged with white above, run strong lines of darker tone. The petals, very narrow at base, are yellowish green, suffused and lined with copper above, paler below. The slipper shows similar colouring.

On the same plant, open at the same time, but from another stem, was a flower of the common Dauthierii type. Still more remarkable, one year this second stem bore a flower of which half the dorsal was pale yellow, the other half coppery green, as is usual, thus betraying a futile inclination to rival its albino sister. The petals were scarcely affected, however.

Dauthierii marmoratum.—Another abnormal form. The point of the dorsal, and the high shoulders, are white, the rest crimson-maroon. From the point descend three or four broad lines, or long splashes, of green, with striking effect. The petals are marbled longitudinally with purple on a dusky ground. The lip is dull, dusky crimson.

Lord Derby (Rothschildianum × superbiens).—An immense flower—the grand dorsal rosy white, tinged with pale green in the middle, pale purple on either hand, dark lines circling upward over all. The petals, outlined with purple at the base, change to pale green, almost to white, below and at the tips. Great spots of darkest crimson stud the whole. Slipper maroon, greenish at the toe.

Evenor (Argus × bellatulum).—Ground-colour throughout ochreous yellow. The dorsal has a purplish base and maroon lines of dots. Broad round petals, closely spotted with maroon. Slipper purplish above, ochre below.

Excelsior (Rothschildianum × Harrisianum).—Dorsal long, high-shouldered, greenish, with darkest crimson edging lines of the same tint, and white margin. Petals depressed, of a like green, crimson along the upper edge, covered with the heavy spots and hairs of Rothschildianum. Slipper very long, dull crimson.

Engelhardtiae (insigne Maulei × Spicerianum).—The dorsal has very broad shoulders, narrowing to a wasp-waist, where the upper white changes abruptly to bright green, spotted with pink. A strong crimson line runs from base to tip. Petals so evenly curved downwards that they seem to make a half-circle, coppery yellow in hue, handsomely gauffered on the upper edge, and lined with copper colour. Immensely wide lip, coppery ochre with a bright green lining.

Edwardii (superbiens × Fairieanum).—Dorsal long, white-edged, stained at the margin with purplish crimson and lined with the same. Short narrow petals, very strongly bowed, greenish, edged throughout with purplish crimson. Slipper green at toe, coppery above.

Fairieanum.—No orchid is so interesting as this in the point of view which may be called historic. In the autumn of 1857, Mr. Reid of Burnham and Mr. Parker, nursery-man, of Holloway, sent flowers of it to Sir W. Hooker at Kew, asking what they might be. Shortly afterwards Mr. Fairie of Liverpool showed a plant in flower at the R.H.S. meeting, and Dr. Lindley named it after him. It is believed that all these plants were bought at Stevens' Sale-rooms among a number of orchids forwarded from Assam. But none have turned up since, and attempts to find the habitat have been totally unsuccessful.

Those who expect to see a flower big in proportion to its fame will be disappointed; but if small, indeed very small, Cyp. Fairieanum is striking both in form and colour. The upstanding dorsal has a crest, from which the sides curl back. Its ground-colour is white with a greenish tinge. Broad lines of maroon fall downwards from the crest, lessening as they go, but multiplying towards the edges, where they form a close network. The petals curl as sharply as a cow's horn, inverted at the tips to show a maroon lining; they are greenish above, with three sharp little maroon bars at the base, and slender lines of maroon; maroon also is the narrow edging. The shield of the column, small as it is, cannot be overlooked, for it shines like a jewel—exquisitely mottled with the brightest green, accentuated by a tiny arch of maroon on either side. Slipper greenish, with blurred lines of maroon.

Gertrude (Chamberlainianum × insigne Chantinii).—Dorsal white above, bright green below, heavily dotted in lines with crimson-brown. Petals finely gauffered, dusky crimson, spotted. The slipper, crimson-purple, looks very bright by contrast.

Tesselatum porphyreum (concolor × barbatum).—The pale ochreous tone of one parent and the purple of the other have produced a very remarkable result in combination. The general effect distinctly red. The round dorsal is reddish above, of a deeper shade at base, with dotted lines of red; the petals curve down, dark red at the base, fading towards the ends, which are clothed in a pretty network of pale red. The green slipper is clouded and netted over with crimson.

Telemachus (niveum × Lawrenceanum).—The dorsal, very broad, is tinged with purple in the centre. Crimson lines ascend from a green base and the margin all round is white. The petals are green, changing to purple, with darker lines and spots. Slipper crimson.

Tautzianum lepidum (niveum × barbatum Warneri).—A rosy flower, covered throughout with lines and network of crimson. The lip darker.

Georges Truffaut (ciliolare × Stonei).—Very large. The tall dorsal has crimson edges and lines, greenish centre. The twisted petals—greenish, with crimson lines, very large maroon spots and crimson-purple tips—hang loosely. An enormous slipper, all crimson-brown.

Mrs. E. G. Uihlein (villosum aureum × Leeanum giganteum).— The dorsal rises to a point between shoulders perfectly square, white, with a heavy slash of copper from base to crest; the centre greenish-coppery, with lines and mottling of pale crimson. Petals green in the upper half, clouded and lined with copper; paler below. Slipper similar.

Venustum (Measures variety).—A remarkable sport. Small. The white dorsal is striped with clear green lines, rising from a green cloud at the base. The ochreous copper petals have a green base. Slipper the same, covered with a pretty green network.

Watsonianum (Harrisianum nigrum × concolor).—The white crested dorsal shows a crimson line in the centre, green on either side, crimson towards the edges. The petals, dark green at base, fade to a paler tint, and the ends are crimson; all softly lined with crimson. Slipper maroon.

Woodlandsense (Dayanum × Javanicum virens).—Among the rare Cypripeds in this collection, I have noted several of which the dorsal sepal bore a cap, elaborate as eccentric in shape. But this is most singular of all. Between the point of the dorsal and the shoulder is a process which I can only describe in architectural language as a volute reversed; an addition so abnormal and inexplicable that I really find nothing to say about it. In other respects the dorsal is striking—handsomely rounded, white with a rosy margin, the vivid green at the base not fading softly but abrupt almost as a splash; petals the same vivid green, with maroon spots and a stain of copper at the ends. The rosy stamenode shows well upon this ground. Slipper pale green, with a pleasing network of copper.

Zeus (tonsum × Boxallii).—The white globular dorsal rises from a very slender green waist, with a broad dark-crimson line up the centre. Petals dark coppery in the upper half, pale below. Slipper dusky.

Annie Measures (bellatulum × Dayanum).—Dorsal yellowish, outlined white, covered with slender purple lines and dots. Large smooth petals, netted over with small crimson dots in a pattern. Slipper narrow, dull crimson above, white toe.

Frau Ida Brandt (Io grande × Youngianum).—The large dorsal, white at the edges, is suffused with green and purple; the long petals, green and purple, are depressed. Heavy spots of crimson-brown, furnished with stiff hairs, cover them. Handsomely reversed at the tip. Slipper greenish-coppery.

Adrastus (Leeanum × Boxallii).—Here the large white dorsal with green base is heavily blotched with red-brown in the centre, lightly at the sides. The closely drooping petals, yellowish green, have the upper half splashed and mottled with a lively brown almost obscuring the ground-colour, which reappears in the lower half. Lip green at toe, coppery above.

Athos (parentage unknown) has an odd colouring—ochreous-green sepals, outlined with white and profusely dotted with brown; petals bright ochre, the upper length scored with lines of raw sienna. The lip similar.

Arthurianum pulchellum (Fairieanum × insigne Chantinii).—

The green dorsal is thickly dotted all over with brown; the tip falls over, showing its white underside. Petals depressed, greenish, charmingly frilled, clouded and lined with copper-brown above, spotted with copper below. Slipper greenish, handsomely veined and marbled in a soft coppery tone.

Astraea (laevigatum × Spicerianum).—Dorsal white, with a pale green base, whence a heavy radius, maroon in colour, mounts to the tip; petals narrow, loosely hanging, greenish at base, crimson-purple through most of their length, marked with red lines. Slipper greenish, stained with purple.

Aurantiacum (venustum × insigne aureum).—Ochreous-green dorsal, its square top broadly crowned with white, spotted below with brownish-red; petals darker, similarly spotted. The slipper harmonises.

Cleopatra (Hookerae × aenanthum superbum).—A striking flower—deep glossy crimson, ribbed with a darker hue. On the upper length of the petals are heavy warts; the lower has a greenish tawny stain at base, like the slipper.

Lily Measures (Dayanum × niveum).—The dorsal is white, daintily flushed, with green base. Lines of red dots ascend from it, growing smaller and fainter as they rise. Such lines form a pleasing network on the petals, which have a yellowish smear at the base. The slipper corresponds.

Lawrebel (Lawrenceanum × bellatulum).—A grand and gorgeous hybrid. The green patch at the base of the dorsal is promptly swallowed up by a crimson cloud, which again fades into a delicious mottling of crimson on a white ground. The petals are vivid green above, paler below, both changing to crimson at the tips. Slipper yellowish at the edge and the toe, crimson between.

Lawrebel (Woodlands variety) shows the difference of colour so often found among seedlings of the same parentage and the same 'batch.' Here the crimson is by no means so bright, in fact purplish, but it covers nearly the whole surface of the dorsal, and what remains is not white but green. On the petals also, which are broader, green occupies nearly all the space, though less vivid, and the crimson of the tips almost disappears. They are heavily spotted with maroon. Slipper dusky purple, netted over with maroon.

La France (nitens × niveum).—White and very graceful. The only trace of colour appears in broad pink spots at the base of the dorsal, and smaller spots, more profuse, at the base of the petals. On the slipper they are smaller still, set along the edge.

Lawrenceanum-Hyeanum has a broad white dorsal, clouded with green at the base, and marked with handsome green lines. The narrow petals stand out firmly, vivid green, with lines of a deeper shade. The slipper also is green but pale. Another example is very much larger.

Lawrenceanum Sir Trevor.—This is no hybrid, but a wonderful variety of the species. The dorsal strangely broad and depressed—squat in fact. White in colour, with superb green lines mounting from the green cloud below, it sits tight over the rectangular petals of dark but vivid green, marked with deeper lines. The slipper is yellowish-green.

Leucochilum giganteum (assumed to be a hybrid of Godefroyae × bellatulum).—A compact flower, of which the three parts seem equal in size. White, with a faint ochreous tinge; covered throughout, saving the margin, with crimson spots, which form almost a blotch in the midst of the dorsal. Slipper small and white.

Leysenianum (barbatum Crossii × bellatulum).—The dorsal is very handsome and striking, bright crimson at top, fading to a dusky base, lined with crimson. The clinging petals, tawny green in the upper length, are washed with crimson in the lower; all profusely spotted with maroon. Slipper dull crimson.

Mrs. Fred Hardy (superbiens × bellatulum).—A very dainty hybrid. The dorsal, white with a greenish centre, is covered with interlacing crimson lines dotted with maroon, saving the clear margin. The petals almost form a semi-circle, greenish with a white edge, netted over with pale crimson and dotted with maroon in lines. The slipper greenish, with a pretty pink network round the upper part.

Holidayanum (concolor × almum).—Excepting a narrow white margin the dorsal is bright crimson, darkening towards the greenish base; petals greenish, with edges and dotted lines of crimson. Slipper dull crimson, with yellowish toe.

Hirsuto-Sallierii.—The upper half of the dorsal is white, the lower clear yellow-green, the whole covered with antlered lines of grass-green; petals yellow-green, finely frilled, tipped with palest purple. Pale purple and greenish also is the slipper.

Mrs. Herbert Measures (Lathamianum × Leeanum giganteum).—The great dorsal, yellow tinged with purple, has the shape of a flattened peg-top. A broad splash of maroon bisects it. The cinnamon-coloured petals are flushed with red, and lined with the same tint; the midrib is maroon. Slipper abnormally wide, purplish.

Javanicum.—A species, named from its habitat. Small and solidly green save the white crest of the dorsal, and the pale purple tips of the narrow petals. Such strong and decided colouring makes it useful to the hybridiser.

Measuresianum (villosum × venustum).—The small triangular

dorsal, white, is evenly striped with green; petals yellow-green, with a grass-green base and emerald lines from end to end. The slipper shows a charming network of vivid green on a tawny yellow ground.

Marchioness of Salisbury (bellatulum × barbatum superbum, Sander's variety).—Dorsal hollow, broadly crimson all round the margin, dusky white inside, striped with crimson and speckled with maroon. Petals closely depressed, white, with a shade of green above, of crimson below, dotted with maroon. Slipper tawny crimson, with clouding of the same.

Marshallianum (venustum-pardinum × concolor).—Unique in effect. Dorsal and petals ochreous white, with a faint crimson flush; all densely covered with minute crimson dots. Slipper of a yellow almost bright.

Brysa (Boissierianum × Sedeni candidulum).—A handsome plant, with long pale leaves. Dorsal greenish, corkscrew petals similar, tinged with pink. Slipper pale pink, all the inside prettily dotted with brown.

Muriel Hollington (niveum × insigne).—A broad flower but compact. The globular white dorsal has a pink cloud at the base and dots of crimson. The petals, similar, have crimson lines. Slipper prettily mottled with pink.

Lavinia (concolor × barbatum).—White of ground-colour all through, with a faintest flush of rose-pink. The whole of the dorsal marked with maroon dots upon regular lines of crimson. The broad drooping petals are spotted irregularly with the same tint. The narrow white slipper has a close array of crimson dots round the edge.

Cydonia (concolor × Curtisii).—Dorsal flesh-colour at the edges; in the middle a broad green stain which fades towards the apex. Midrib brown-crimson, with a paler network of the same over all. Petals crimson above, then greenish, pink or light crimson below, with faint lines and sharp little dots of crimson-brown. Slipper brownish and green.

Symonsianum (volonteanum × Rothschildianum).—Impressive for size and width, but not brilliant nor attractive in colour. Dorsal greenish, with pink-flushed edges, marked by strong lines of crimson-brown. Petals greenish, tipped with pale crimson, strongly dotted along the edges with the bristling tufts of Rothschildianum. Slipper nondescript—greenish and purplish.

J. Coles (Godefrovae-leucochilum majesticum × Dayanum superbum).—A charming flower. The dorsal is purplish crimson, with a pretty tinge of green in the midst and narrow white edges; the whole lined and netted over with crimson-purple. Petals the same, very dark at base, paling to a greenish centre; all closely

132

spotted with the dark crimson tone. Slipper maroon, highly polished.

Princess May (callosum × Sanderianum).—A stately bloom, of impressive colouring. The tall bulbous dorsal is white at the crest, crimson-lake below, pale green at base; the whole striped with maroon and with crimson dots. Petals long, drooping far below the greenish slipper, green in the midst, with crimson edges and profuse dottings of crimson.

Pylaeus (Cardinale × Sedeni).—Pink and pretty. The pointed dorsal is pale pink above, greenish in the midst. The sharp pink petals have edges of carmine, and carmine tips. The pouch-like slipper is crimson; its lining ivory, marbled with pink.

Phoebe (laevigatum × bellatulum).—Rosy-white throughout. The dorsal bears a cloud of crimson-lake, sharply defined, darkening to maroon at the base, whence proceed heavy branching lines of crimson and maroon. The petals, crimson-stained above, heavily dotted all over with maroon, have white margins. Slipper bright crimson at the top, whitish below.

Paris (bellatulum × Stonei).—A grand beauty. The broad globular dorsal has a greenish patch in the midst, surrounded by purple, netted all over with maroon lines. The edges are pure white, as distinct as if drawn with the brush. Petals depressed, curiously blunted at the tips, verdigris-green at base, fading and changing to dusky crimson, with heavy spots of deepest maroon. Slipper purple, netted over with carmine; yellowish at the toe.

Rowena (Chamberlainianum × bellatulum).—Dorsal greenish-yellow above, darkest maroon below; branching maroon lines circle upwards. Petals greenish towards the tips, clouded at base, edged, scored, and dotted all over with maroon-crimson. The shield of the column intensely dark maroon and shining. Slipper striped with a pleasant pale crimson, and closely speckled over with tiny points of a darker shade.

Mrs. W. A. Roebling (caudatum × leucorrhodum).—The colouring is very delicate. Dorsal long, with a twisted crest; all stainless grass-green. Petals, which make one complete revolution or twist, softly greenish in the middle, edged with tender pale crimson, which also appears on the reverse; the lower base shows a brilliant decoration of tiny crimson bars round the column. The pouched slipper, bright pink, has a yellow lining, freckled with greenish dots.

Reticulatum.—A species, known also as Boissierianum, as curious as charming. The dorsal, of extraordinary length and the same narrow width throughout, curls over at the crest—bright pea-green, with slender lines a shade darker. The petals have the same

133

slender green lines; they are very thin, closely and evenly twisted in six complete spirals. The shield of the column intensely dark green. Slipper green, its lining snow-white, with purple dots.

Charles Richmond (bellatulum × barbatum superbum).—The broad purplish dorsal has a whitish outline and a greenish tinge in the centre; its midrib is very strong purple, as are the lines which intersect it. Petals purple, darker at the base, dotted all over with maroon. Slipper dark purplish-crimson. In colour, shape, and size alike this hybrid is most impressive.

Schofieldianum (bellatulum × hirsutissimum).—Very distinct. On a yellowish-white ground the dorsal has a pale greenish centre, surrounded by purple, deepening at the base; all scored with branching lines of purple in dots. The petals are broad and strong, yellowish-white, tinged with purple, closely covered with maroon-purple dots. Slipper purplish-crimson, greenish at the toe.

Southgatense (callosum × bellatulum).—The dorsal has a rosy-white ground, very heavily clouded with dark crimson below, and almost hidden by strong lines of crimson and maroon. The petals have a touch of bright green at the base, edges of a lively dark crimson, and strong dots of maroon. Slipper crimson, dusky yellow at the toe.

Southgatense superbum.—This is another example of the difference which seedlings from the same pod may display; cases even more striking could be adduced with ease. Incomparably finer than the last. The rosy-white dorsal is stained with crimson up to the edges, and scored with darker lines. The petals, slightly greenish at the base, have a dotting of crimson on their rosy-white ground. The slipper, whitish, is prettily speckled with crimson round the top.

Massaianum (superciliare × Rothschildianum).—A large bold flower. Dorsal white, greenish in the middle. Clear thin lines of purple, almost black, alternate with lines equally thin of pale green. The fine long petals are greenish above, palest purple below, with the massive spots of Rothschildianum. Strong hairs line the edges. The broad shield is dusky ochre. Slipper maroon, netted over with a deeper shade.

Miss Clara Measures (bellatulum eximium × barbatum grandiflorum).—Lively dark crimson. The crest of the dorsal is handsomely defined by semicircular scallops on each side. Petals depressed, clinging to the slipper, greenish at base, fading and changing to the same bright dark crimson as the dorsal; all speckled finely in a deeper shade. Slipper crimson. A grand flower.

Measuresiae (bellatulum × superbiens).—Dorsal rosy, with green tip and a faintly green centre, dotted over with maroon in lines. Petals rosy white, tinged with purple above, strongly speckled with maroon. Slipper crimson, fading towards the toe, covered with crimson dots.

Winifred Hollington (niveum × callosum).—Dorsal pale dusky crimson, purple at base; lines of the same colour, accentuated by dots. The handsome petals are pale purple, with darker branching lines and specks over all. Slipper purplish, with pale crimson lines.

Nitidum (selligerum majus × nitens).—Very large. The broad white edges of the dorsal fold sharply back. It is green in the midst, with green lines and longitudinal rows of strong dark brown spots. Petals clear brown above, with a tinge of maroon, paler below, with spots of the same. Slipper brownish. The whole polished and shiny to a degree which gives it the name nitidum.

But there was one astonishing peculiarity in the flower which I saw—the first produced. Everyone knows that in the genus Cypripedium the two lower sepals are fused together, making a single limb, small commonly, insignificant, and nearly hidden by the slipper. But in this case there was no attempt at fusion. The lower sepals stood out as clearly as in a Cattleya, one on each side the slipper—whitish, with green lines and crimson spots at the base. It will be interesting to observe whether this deformity—which is in truth a return to the more graceful pristine form—will prove to be permanent.

Sir Redvers Buller.—A new hybrid of which the parents are understood to be Lucie × insigne; the former itself a hybrid—Lawrenceanum × ciliolare. I have not seen the flower, which is thus described in the Gardeners' Chronicle, Jan. 20, 1900: 'The fine dorsal is of a pale-green tint in the lower half with dark chocolate-purple dotted lines; the upper portion pure white, with the basal dark lines continued into it, but of a deep rose-purple. The petals are yellowish, tinged with rose on the outer halves and blotched with dark purplish chocolate. Lip greenish with the face tinged reddish-brown.'

STORY OF CYPRIPEDIUM PLATYTAENIUM

This is the rarest and costliest of all orchids—of all flowers that blow, indeed, and all green things, from the cedar of Lebanon to the hyssop upon the housetop. I think it no exaggeration to say that a strong specimen would be worth its weight in diamonds if a little one—for the most enthusiastic of millionaires seem to lose courage when biddings go beyond a certain sum. But it is long since any plants came into the market.

I suppress part of the name, as usual, fearing to daunt casual readers. Be it understood that this treasure is a variety of Cypripedium Stoneii; the specific title should be introduced in speaking of it. Doubtless platytaenium is a very handsome member of the family, impressive in size and shape, elegantly coloured. But one who regards the flower with eyes undazzled by fashion may pronounce that its value lies mostly in its renown.

But one plant has ever been discovered; and that came to Europe unannounced. Messrs. Low sold a quantity of a new Cypripedium from Borneo. Some pieces were bought by Mr. Day, of Tottenham, at an average of eight shillings each. They flowered successively, and Mr. Day named the species Stoneii, after his excellent gardener. In 1863, however, one appeared different to the rest—different, as it has proved, to all the myriads which have been discovered since. This was named platytaenium. But besides the merit of rarity, it is distinguished by a peculiar slowness of growth. Mr. Day multiplied the specimen as fast as he could, but between 1863 and 1881 he only succeeded in making four small plants from it. One of these was sold to Mrs. Morgan, of New York; it perished, doubtless, for when, at her death, a Cypriped was put up under that hallowed name, and bought at a long price, it proved to be the common Stoneii. Mr. Dorman, of Sydenham, was the victim. I may mention that two of the largest orchid-dealers in Europe sent an agent expressly to buy this 'lot' in New York. Mr. Day then had three left. One of them he divided, and gave a fragment to his sister, Mrs. Wolstenholme. The Tottenham collection was dispersed in 1881; Mr. Day kept one small plant, Baron Schröder bought one for £106; Mr. Lee, of Leatherhead, and Sir Trevor Lawrence, in partnership, one for £147. Three or four years afterwards this was divided, each partner taking his share. Baron Schröder afterwards bought Mr. Lee's. Also he bought the one Mr. Day kept back, for £159:12s., at the death of that gentleman. Then Mrs. Wolstenholme's executors put up her example—which had never flowered—and Baron

Schröder secured it for £100. These prices do not seem to bear out my statement that platytaenium is the most valuable of all orchids. Infinitely greater sums have been paid. But it must be remembered that these were all tiny bits, weakened by division whenever they grew big enough to cut. At present Baron Schröder and Sir Trevor Lawrence have all the stock existing, to human knowledge. How much either would obtain at Protheroe's for his little hoard makes a favourite theme for speculation in a gathering of orchidists. They have one significant hint to go upon. Two years ago Mr. Ames, of Boston, U.S.A., commissioned Mr. Sander to offer Sir Trevor Lawrence a cheque of 800 guineas for one plant. And Sir Trevor declined it.

Now for the legend. That consignment of Cyp. Stoneii in which platytaenium appeared was forwarded by Sir Hugh Low from Sarawak. He recalls the circumstances with peculiar distinctness, as is natural. The plants were collected on the very top of a limestone hill at Bidi, near Bau, famous afterwards in the annals of Sarawak as the spot whence the Chinese insurgents started to overthrow the government of Rajah Brooke. But the gold washings had not been discovered then. Such Chinamen as dwelt in the neighbourhood were mostly gardeners and small traders. A few sought nuggets in holes and fissures of the limestone, and found them, too, occasionally. Sir Hugh Low could never frame a satisfactory explanation of the presence of gold under such conditions, but it is frequent in Borneo. That auriferous strata should decompose, and that nuggets should be transferred to another formation during the process, is easily intelligible. But in many instances, as at Bau, the gold is found at a considerable height, and no trace remains of those loftier hills from which it must have fallen. Deposits of tin occur under just the same circumstances in the Malay Peninsula.

The top of this little hill was a basin, much like a shallow crater, encircled by jagged peaks as by a wall. Each of these was clothed in the glossy leaves of Cyp. Stoneii from top to bottom, as it would be with ivy in our latitude. So easy was orchid-collecting in those days. Sir Hugh had but to choose the finest, and pull off as many as his servants could carry. In the hollow of the basin other Cypripeds were growing—plants with spotted foliage—and he has not ceased to regret leaving these untouched, since wider knowledge inclines him to fancy that they belonged to species not yet introduced. At one spot, however, beneath the shadow of the little peaks, gold-seekers made a practice of camping. Ashes lay thick there, and bits of charcoal and dry bones. Here sprang a single tuft of Cyp. Stoneii, and in passing Sir Hugh was tempted to dig it up. He cherishes a suspicion—which he does not attempt to justify, of course—that this solitary plant, growing under conditions so different to the rest, was platytaenium.

Some years afterwards, a young clerk in the service of a German firm at Singapore, visited Sarawak on his holiday. Orchids made a standing topic for conversation in that early time. He heard much about Mr. Day's priceless Cypriped at the capital, and he resolved to try his luck. I may call him Smidt for convenience; my informants are not sure of the name, after a lapse of forty years.

There is no trouble in reaching Bau. The village stands on the river Sarawak, and at any moment of the day a sampan can be hired to take one thither. Smidt did not travel in luxury. If he kept a 'boy' at Singapore, like a thrifty young Teuton he left him behind. Servants are as easily found in those countries as sampans, if one be not too particular. Smidt engaged a Chinaman who had good recommendations, though not of recent date, nor from persons living in Sarawak; he had come thither from Penang to 'better himself,' as he said, and had been working at the gold-fields. For convenience again we may give him a name—Ahtan.

The project of visiting Bau was not agreeable to this Chinaman. 'I makee bad pigeon there one time,' he said frankly. But the objection was not serious.

Bau had changed since Sir Hugh Low's day. In the meantime the Dutch authorities at Sambas had irritated the gold-diggers of that region to the point that they massacred a body of troops—I do not mean to hint that the Dutch policy was unjustifiable. In consequence a great number of Chinamen fled across the frontier, found profitable washings at Bau, and invited their comrades. So many came, and they showed such a lawless spirit from the outset, that the Rajah's government took alarm. But as yet all was quiet enough.

Smidt had obtained a note from one of the Chinese merchants at Sarawak, with whom his employers did business, to the head of the Kunsi—the Gold-diggers' Union, as we should say. That personage invited him to use his house. Unwillingly did Ahtan accompany his master. He bowed before the Kunsi chief, and made a long discourse with downcast eyes and folded hands. The chief answered shortly and motioned him to go about his business.

If Smidt made inquiries about that wonderful organisation, the Kunsi of the gold-diggers at Bau, so soon to be crushed in a mad revolt, assuredly he found matter to interest him. The parent society in Sambas has annals dating back two hundred years, and its system was imported, they say, from China without alteration. There is no reason to doubt the statement. Anyhow, we find among these immigrants, two centuries ago, a perfected system of trade union, benefit clubs, life assurance, co-operative stores, and provision for old age, such as British working-men may contemplate with puzzled and envious despair at the present day. Every detail is so well adjusted—by the experience of ages—that disputes scarcely ever arise; when they do the Council gives judgment, and no one questions its decision. The earnings of the whole body are stored in the Treasury. There is a general meeting once a fortnight, when the accounts are audited in public, and each member receives his share as per scale, subject to the deduction for veterans' past work, widows and orphans, and also for the goods he has bought at the co-operative store. But I must not linger on this fascinating theme.

Next day Smidt started to explore the famous hill with Ahtan, who carried the tambok—the luncheon basket. He found Cypripeds beyond counting and noted certain spots to be re-visited. Then he chose a shady nook for lunch, and Ahtan lit a fire.

It was beneath a wall of limestone, a tangle of foliage above, where the sunlight struck it, but clothed only in moss and ferns and bare roots in the shade below. There was wind upon the hill as usual, and Ahtan made his fire in a cleft.

Smith sat on a log opposite, smoking, after the meal. He remembered afterwards that Ahtan was eager to start, packing his utensils hastily, and predicting 'muchee rain by'm bye minute.' But no signs of change were visible. Presently the Chinaman put a quantity of green leaves upon the fire. Such a volume of smoke arose as called Smidt's attention.

It was in a cleft, and he sat opposite, as has been said. The blaze had scorched that drapery of ferns. The moss just above had peeled off in flakes, taken fire mostly and dropped. So in places the rock stood bare. Looking in that direction now, Smidt observed a yellow gleam, hidden by smoke for a moment, then reappearing more distinctly. It was worth investigation. He rose leisurely and crossed the little space. Ahtan was standing on one side. As he scattered the fire with his foot, looking for that yellow gleam the while, a tremendous blow felled him. He was dimly conscious of another before his senses fled.

Not till sunset did Smidt feel strong enough to descend the hill; before starting he looked for the 'yellow gleam'—it had vanished, and in place of it was a hole. Bloodstained and tottering he regained the public path. Diggers returning from their work laughed heartily at the spectacle, but perhaps they meant no harm. Chinamen must not be judged by the laws that apply to other mortals. At least they warned the chief, who sent two stalwart members of the Kunsi to assist his guest. They also found the situation vastly amusing, but they were kind enough.

The chief had a bottle of skimpin ready. He set a slave to wash Smidt's head, and clothed him in a snowy bajo. No questions did he ask. Smidt told his short story, and begged him to pursue the malefactor.

'No good, sir,' said the chief. 'I policeman here—I know. Where you think Ahtan?'

'In the jungle, I suppose, making for Kuching with the great nugget he picked out of the rock. Send to warn the Tuan magistrate, at least.'

'I say, sir, I Tuan magistrate here, and I know.' He unlocked a coffer, iron-bound, using three separate keys; brought out a parcel wrapped in cloth and slowly unfolded it, looking at Smidt the while, his narrow eyes twinkling.

'You say nugget, hey?'

Smidt gasped. It was a lump of gold as big as his two fists.

'Is this—is this mine?'

The chief sat down to laugh and rolled about, spluttering Chinese interjections.

'Is this mine? He-he-he-he! Mine? This gold, sir! Kunsi take gold—all gold here! You says, mine, sir? Ha! ha! ha!'

Smidt did not feel assured of his legal rights.

'You took it from Ahtan?' he asked. 'Did you arrest him?'

The chief had another fit. Recovering, he answered, 'Ahtan down this way,' and stamped upon the ground.

'In the cellar? Oh, that's a comfort! I'll carry him to Kuching to-morrow.'

This caused another outburst of merriment. 'I tell, sir, I Tuan magistrate at Bau. Ahtan he under order for kingdom come to-night.'

This was rather shocking. 'Oh, I don't ask that. He must be tried.'

'What your matter, sir?' the chief snapped out. 'I try him, and I say die! Ahtan is Kunsi man. He play trick before—I let him go. We catch him on river with gold. He die this time.'

Doubtless he did—not for attempted murder, but for breaking his oath to the Kunsi. Smidt ought to have denounced this monstrous illegality to the Rajah. But his firm did a great business with Chinamen, and their secret societies have a very long arm. I imagine that he held his tongue.

STORY OF CYPRIPEDIUM SPICERIANUM

The annals of Cypripedium Spicerianum open in 1878, when Mrs. Spicer, a lady residing at Wimbledon, asked Messrs. Veitch to come and see a curious flower, very lovely, as she thought, which had made its appearance in her green-house. Messrs. Veitch came; with no extravagant hopes perhaps, for experience might well make them distrustful of feminine enthusiasm. But in this instance it was more than justified, and, in short, they carried off the marvel, leaving a cheque for seventy guineas behind. I may remark that Cypripeds are easy to cultivate. They are also quick to increase. Messrs. Veitch hurried their specimen along, and divided it as fast as was safe. To say that the morsels fetched their weight in gold would be the reverse of exaggeration—mere bathos.

Importers sat up. They were not without a hint to direct their search in this case. The treasure had arrived amongst a quantity of Cyp. insigne. Therefore it must be a native of the Himalayan region—Assam, Darjeeling, or Sikkim, no doubt. There are plenty of persons along that frontier able and willing to hunt up a new plant. A good many of them probably received commissions to find Cypripedium Spicerianum.

At St. Albans they were more deliberate. It is not exactly usual for ladies residing at Wimbledon to receive consignments of orchids. When such an event happens, one may conclude that they have relatives or intimate friends in the district where those orchids grow; it will hardly be waste of time anyhow to inquire. A discreet investigation proved that this lady's son was a tea-planter, with large estates on the confines of Bhutan. With the address in his pocket Mr. Forstermann, a collector of renown, started by next mail.

Orchids must be classed with ferae naturae in which a landowner has no property. But it is not to be supposed that a man of business will tell the casual inquirer where to pick up, on his own estate, weeds worth seventy guineas each. Forstermann did not expect it. Leaving his baggage at the dak bungalow, he strolled afoot to the large and handsome mansion indicated. Mr. Spicer was sitting in the verandah, and in the pleasant, easy way usual with men who very rarely see a white stranger of respectable appearance, he shouted:

'Are you looking for me, sir? Come up!'

Forstermann went up, took an arm-chair and a cheroot, accepted a comforting glass, and sketched his experiences of the road before declaring even his name. Then he announced himself as an aspirant tea-planter, desirous to gain some practical knowledge of the business before risking his very small capital. In short, could Mr. Spicer give him a 'job'?

'I'm afraid not,' said Mr. Spicer. 'We have quite as many men in your position as we can find work for. But anyhow you can look round and talk to our people and see whether the life is likely to suit you. Meantime, you're very welcome to stay here as my guest. If you've brought a gun, my manager will show you some sport; but he's away just now. Oh, you needn't thank me. In my opinion it's the duty of men who have succeeded to help beginners along, and I'm sorry I can't do more for you.'

Forstermann remembers a twinge of conscience here. It may be indubitable that orchids are ferae naturae. But they have a distinct money value for all that, and to remove them from the estate of a man who gives you a reception like this! Anyhow, he felt uncomfortable. But to find the thing was his first duty. Possibly some arrangement might be made, though he could not imagine how.

The invitation was accepted, of course, and a week passed very pleasantly. But Forstermann could not bring his host to the point desired. Several times they observed Cypripedium insigne whilst riding or driving about the neighbourhood. Mr. Spicer even remarked, when his attention was called to it, that he had sent a number of plants home; but nothing followed. Then the manager returned, and the same night an appointment was made to go after duck on the morrow.

Forstermann turned out at dawn, but his companion was not ready. He gave the explanation as they rode along.

'We had another chelan last night—you have learnt the meaning of that word, I daresay!—a faction fight among our people. The coolies on this estate come mostly from Chota Nagpore, and thereabouts. They're good workers, and not so troublesome as regular Hindus when once they've settled down. But there's generally a bother when a new gang arrives. We tell our agents to be very careful in recruiting none but friendly clans. Young Mice and Fig Leaves we find best among the Oraons, Stars and Wild Geese among the Sonthals.' Forstermann was puzzled, but he did not interrupt. 'It's no use, however. They take any fellow that comes along—and between ourselves, you know, considering how many of those scamps bolt with the contract-money and never enlist a soul, we haven't so very much to complain of. It's a bad system, sir!

'Well, when they get here, a mixed lot, they find half a dozen mixed lots established. We have, to my knowledge,' reckoning on his fingers, 'Tortoises, Tigers, Crows, Eels, Grass-spiders, Fishing-

142

nets—ay, and a lot more, besides Stars and Wild-geese. Of course, they quarrel at sight, and we don't interfere unless the chelan gets serious. What's the good? But, besides that, there is a standing provocation, as you may say. Some of our coolies have been with us many years. They don't care to go home—for reasons good, no doubt, but it's not our business. Well, two of these fellows have married—one, a Potato, has married the Stomach of a pig——'

'Eh?' Forstermann could not contain himself.

'Those are their families, you know.' The manager, quite grave hitherto, laughed out suddenly. 'Of course, it seems mighty droll to you, but we're accustomed to it. Each clan claims to be descended from the thing after which it is named. You mustn't ask me how the Stomach of a pig can have children. That's beyond our understanding. The point is that certain of these stocks may not intermarry under pain of death—that's their law. So you may fancy the rumpus when strange Potatoes arriving here find one of their breed——' he laughed again. 'It does sound funny, when you think of it! Last night, however, when the usual disturbance broke out—a new gang arrived yesterday, you know—Minjar, the Eel, who is the other fellow that has married some girl he ought not to, declared he had made blood-brotherhood with the chief of the Bhutias across the river, who would come to avenge him if he were hurt. And I fancy that's not quite such nonsense as you would think. I saw Minjar there that time I got the orchid——'

Forstermann heard no more of the tale. The orchid! They reached the pool, and he shot ducks conscientiously, but his thoughts were busy in devising means to lead the conversation back to that point.

There was no need of finesse, however. At a word the manager told everything. He it was who found the Cypripedium which had caused such a fuss, when shooting on the other side of the river—that is, beyond British territory. Struck with its beauty, he gathered a plant or two and gave them to Mr. Spicer. It took him several days' journey to reach the spot, but he was shooting by the way. Tigers abounded there—so did fever. The mountaineers were as unfriendly as they dared to be. For these reasons Mr. Spicer begged him not to return. The same motive, doubtless, caused the planter to be reticent towards others.

With a clear conscience and heartiest thanks Forstermann bade his host farewell next day. He had a long and painful search before him still, for his informant could give no more than general directions. The plant grew upon rocks along the bed of a stream to the north-west of Mr. Spicer's plantation, not less than two days'

143

journey from the river—that was about all. The inhabitants of the country, besides tigers, were savages.

Many a stream did Forstermann explore under the most uncomfortable circumstances, wading thigh-deep, hour after hour, day after day. I am sorry that I have not room even to summarise the long letter in which he detailed those adventures.

To search the upland waters would have been comparatively easy; he might have walked along the bank. But the Cypripedium grew in a valley; and nowhere is tropical vegetation more dense than in those steaming clefts which fall from the mountains of Bhutan. To cut a path was out of the question; the work would have lasted for months, putting expense aside. It was necessary to march up the bed of the stream.

Forstermann ascended each tributary with patient hopefulness, knowing that success was certain if he could hold out. And it came at length to one so deserving; but the manager had wandered to a much greater distance than he thought. After wading all the forenoon up a torrent which had not yet lost its highland chill, Forstermann reached a glade, encircled by rocks steep as a wall—so steep that he had to fashion rakes of bamboo wherewith to drag down the masses of orchid which clung to them. It was Cypripedium Spicerianum!

Then arose the difficulty of getting his plunder away. After much journeying to and fro, Forstermann engaged thirty-two Bhutias, half of them to carry rice for the others along those mountain tracks, where 25 lbs. is a heavy load. So they travelled until, one day, after halting at a village, the men refused to advance. The road ahead was occupied by a tiger—I should mention that such alarms had been incessant; in no country are tigers so common or so dangerous as in Bhutan. Forstermann drove them along; at the next bit of jungle eight threw down their loads and vanished. He found himself obliged to return, but eight more were missing when he reached the village. There was no other road. Gradually the poor fellow perceived that he must abandon his enterprise or clear the path. At sunset, they told him, the brute would be watching— probably in a tree, described with precision. Forstermann spent the time in writing farewell letters—making his will, perhaps. Towards sunset, he took a rifle and a gun and sallied forth.

The Bhutias assured him that there was no danger—from this enemy, at least—until he reached the neighbourhood of the tree; but we may imagine the terrors of that lonely walk, which must be repeated in darkness, if he lived, or if the tiger did not show. But luck did not desert a man so worthy of favour. He recognised the tree, an old dead stump overhanging the path, clothed in ferns and

144

creepers. Surveying it as steadily as the tumult of his spirits would allow, in the fading light he traced a yellow glimmer among the leaves. Through his field-glass, at twenty yards' distance, he scrutinised this faint shadow. The tiger grew impatient—softly it raised its head—so softly behind that screen of ferns that a casual wayfarer would not have noticed it. But it was the hint Forstermann needed. With a prayer he took aim, fired—threw down his rifle and snatched the gun. But crash—stone-dead fell the tiger, and its skin is a hearthrug on which I stood to hear this tale.

So on March 9, 1884, 40,000 plants of Cypripedium Spicerianum were offered at Stevens' Auction Rooms.

THE COOL HOUSE

Contains about three thousand plants, mostly Odontoglossums. It is a 'lean-to,' of course. Not all the most successful growers use this form of building. Baron Schröder's world-famous Odontoglots dwell in an oblong structure which receives an equal quantity of light from every side. Even the hardiest of epiphytal orchids are conscious of influences which we cannot grasp, and those who understand them are unwilling to lay down fixed rules. But experience shows that under ordinary conditions cool species thrive in a 'lean-to' better than in a house of full span. It may be because the back wall retains moisture and gives it out all day steadily, whilst the air is saturated and dried by turns if fully exposed to a hot sun. Or it may be because the full light of a span-roof is too strong in most situations. A collector once told me that he often found Odontoglossum Pescatorei so buried in Lycopodium as to be invisible until the flower-spike appeared. Evidently such a plant does not need strong light. Both causes operate, perhaps. At least the broad fact is so well established that one might almost fancy Baron Schröder's Odontoglots would do better, if that were possible, in a 'lean-to.'

There are three glass partitions, but from either door the full length of the house is seen; a pleasing vista even when there are no flowers—all smoothly green on one hand, rocky bank upon the other, studded with ferns and creepers and an orchid here and there. Why these plants dislike to stand in a long house open from end to end is a question none the less puzzling because every gardener is ready to explain it. Loving fresh air so well they cannot object to the brisker circulation. But their whims must be respected, and after building a house ninety feet long we must divide it into compartments.

I name a few among the rarities here. Of Odontoglots:—

Wilckeanum.—Upon internal evidence Reichenbach pronounced this a natural hybrid of Od. crispum × Od. luteo-purpureum. It was one among innumerable instances of his sagacity. A few years ago M. Leroy, gardener of Baron Edmond de Rothschild at Armainvilliers, crossed those two species and the flower appeared in 1890. It was Od. Wilckeanum; but for the sake of convenience this garden hybrid is called Leroyanum.

Wilckeanum pallens.—A form still rarer of this rare variety; yellow-ivory in colour, heavily splashed with brown; lip white, with a brown bar across the centre.

Wilckeanum albens.—Very large, white instead of yellowish; spotted and blotched with brown.

Ruckerianum.—Sepals and petals white in the centre, edged with violet, yellow lip; all spotted with reddish-brown.

Ruckerianum splendens.—Larger and more finely coloured in all respects than the normal form. The violet margin is broader.

Vuylstekeanum.—Those who saw the original plant of this noble species at the Temple Show some years since have not forgotten the spectacle assuredly. Petals and dorsal sepal pale yellow; lip and side sepals brightest deepest orange.

Mulus.—A natural hybrid of Od. luteo-purpureum with Od. gloriosum no doubt. It bears a strong spike, branched, with many large flowers, bright yellow blotched with pale brown. But the colouring varies greatly.

Josephinae.—Named after Miss Josephine Measures. White, with a rosy flush; sepals and petals spotted with chocolate at the base.

Hunnewellianum.—Small, but very pretty. Sepals and petals pale yellow, profusely dotted with brown; lip white, with a single brown spot.

Elegans.—Assumed to be a natural hybrid of Od. cirrhosum and Od. Hallii. The ground colour, faintly yellow, is almost concealed by chocolate spots and patches; lip white, with a large blotch in the centre.

Crispum virginale.—Very large and pure white, saving the yellow crest.

Crispum Measuresiae.—Sepals and petals broad, white, spotted and blotted with reddish brown. Lip unusually large, with a single great brown blotch.

Edithae.—Rosy white of sepal and petal, bordered with yellow and barred with chestnut; lip pale yellow, much deeper at the base, with chestnut spots in the centre.

Crispum Our Empress.—A remarkable variety. Very large, rose colour, heavily blotched with reddish purple; lip paler, covered with brown spots.

Crispum Woodlandsense.—A superb example of the 'round-flowering' type. Sepals and petals very broad, densely spotted with cinnamon-brown; lip short, broad, similarly spotted.

Crispum magnificum.—Sepals pale rose; petals and lip very faintly flushed; the whole covered with brown spots.

Bictoniense album.—The ordinary Bictoniense is pretty enough when the lower blooms on the densely clothed spike can be persuaded to last until those above them open. This uncommon sport is much more effective, with sepals and petals of a lively brown, and broad lip of purest white.

Facetum.—A good example of this catches the eye at once. Ground colour pale yellow, almost hidden by great brown bars upon the sepals. The petals are sharply freckled with brown, and up the middle runs a series of dark red dots. Lip similarly freckled above, with a large splash of brown in front; the lip handsomely fringed.

Cristatellum.—Rather small and not impressive, but valuable for its scarcity. The yellow ground colour shows itself only in a few narrow streaks upon sepal and petal, and in the base of the lip. Elsewhere it is hidden beneath layers of chestnut.

Hallii magnificum.—A variety finer in all respects than the common type. Sepals brown, save the yellow tips, and a few yellow lines; petals yellow, with two large brown blots. The fringed lip also is yellow, with two brown blots.

Madrense.—Named after its place of birth, the Sierra Madre, in Mexico. The plant is not uncommon, but it does not flower willingly, as a rule. Sepals and petals are white, with a double purple blotch at the base; lip small, bright orange.

Polyxanthum magnificum.—The grandest variety of a species always treasured. In colour deepest 'old gold,' with four or five great blots of chestnut on the sepals, and as many spots at the base of the petals. The lip has a shallow fringe and a broad splash in the centre.

Wallisii.—Small. Sepals and petals dusky yellow, with a long straight bar of chocolate down the middle. Lip white at the base, with small rosy streaks; the disc rosy, edged with white.

Hallii leucoglossum.—One of the largest Odontoglots. Buff or greenish yellow, lip white, fringed; all heavily blotched and spotted with dark brown.

Mirandum.—Among so many charming species this must be reckoned curious rather than pretty. Narrow and rather small, dull greenish yellow, with a longitudinal bar and spots of red-brown.

Wilckeanum Rothschildianum.—-Perhaps the handsomest form of this rare variety. Large, very broad of sepal and petal, pale yellow, blotched and spotted with brown.

Pescatorei Germinyanum.—Named after the Comte de Germiny, an enthusiastic lover of orchids, as indeed of all other flowers. This ranks among the prettiest forms of Pescatorei. Petals white, sepals flushed; both marked with a spot of dark rose. Lip white, with similar dots.

Sceptrum.—A superb variety of the common luteo-purpureum. Sepals deep reddish brown, with yellow edges; petals yellow, blotched with reddish-brown. Lip yellow, with a single blotch in front.

Coronarium.—One of the Odontoglots which may be termed climbing par excellence, for the pseudo-bulbs thrust out a long shaft before taking form. It makes a very large plant, and probably the example here is the largest existing—at least there are few as big. By successive enlargements, the basket in which it stands has reached the dimensions of three feet by two. Coronarium is reckoned among the species slow to flower, but here we find no difficulty at all. Last season our plant made nine growths and threw up eight spikes—a record! Noble spikes they are too, bearing twenty to thirty blooms; petals of the brightest red-copper, marbled with yellow at the base; petals somewhat browner, both edged with gold. Lip small, narrow, light red, broadening towards the tip, which is pale primrose. I should describe coronarium as the most majestic of Odontoglots.

Crispum Arthurianum.—A notable variety—very large, blush-white, with one enormous chocolate blot and two or three small spots on sepal and petal. Spotted lip.

Crispo-Harryanum.—This is one of the very few hybrid Odontoglots. It was commonly assumed until a few years ago that the genus would not bear fruitful seed in Europe. This notion proves to be ill-founded happily, but to obtain good seed is still very difficult, and to rear the young plants more difficult still. Crispo-Harryanum was raised by M. Chas. Vuylsteke near Ghent. The flowers show the influence of either parent in colour and shape; the petals, which in Harryanum refuse to expand, are almost as flat as in crispum.

Humeanum.—We may confidently assume that this is a natural hybrid of Od. Rossii and Od. cordatum. The former parent is so handsome that he has begotten a very pretty progeny, though the mother is so plain—sepals primrose, closely spotted with brown, petals and lip white, the former similarly spotted at the base.

Tripudians oculatum.—A rare and beautiful variety of an interesting species. Very much larger than the common form; sepals of a lively brown, with yellow tips, petals yellow, mottled with brown; lip white, with violet spots above, a large blot below.

Platycheilum.—One of the oddest and rarest Odontoglots. Sepals and petals white, with a few brown dots at the base; lip large and widespread, pink, spotted with crimson.

Baphicanthum.—A valuable hybrid of Od. crispum and Od. odoratum or Od. gloriosum, as internal evidence suggests. All primrose of ground colour, but the sepals and petals are thickly dotted with red-brown.

Schillerianum.—Exceedingly rare. Pale yellow; sepals and petals spotted with chestnut. The lip has one large chestnut splash in the centre.

Murrellianum.—Probably a natural hybrid of Od. Pescatorei and Od. naevium. White tinged with violet, sepals and petals spotted with purple.

Lindeni.—A superb species, but uncommonly reluctant to display its charms, as a rule. In my own poor little house it has been growing bigger for years and years. The pseudo-bulbs are five inches high now, and more than two thick, but I look for flowers in vain. When they condescend to appear they are all sulphur-yellow, crumpled, or, as the phrase goes, undulated, in a fashion quite unlike any other Odontoglot.

Grande magnificum.—The common form of grande ranks among the showiest of flowers, much too big, indeed, and too strong in colour, to be approved by a dainty taste. But this is even bigger, its yellow more brilliant, its red-brown markings more distinctly red. There is record of sixteen flowers on one spike, each seven inches across!—I scarcely expect to be believed, but 'chapter and verse' are forthcoming on demand.

Crispum aureum.—Almost as yellow as polyxanthum, 'the very golden'—a most remarkable variety. The spots are few and small.

Crispum Cooksoni, on the other hand, is white, superbly spotted, or rather blotched, with crimson brown. Perhaps the best of its class.

Crispum Reginae.—Immense. White. The handsome spots, of purplish brown, are more regularly disposed than usual.

Crispum Chestertoni.—Peculiar for a yellow lip, while sepals and petals are white; the former of these heavily splashed, and the latter sprinkled, with red-brown. The lip has a brown blot on the disc.

Rossii aspersum is a natural hybrid of Od. Rossii and Od. maculatum, as is supposed. Sepals and petals faintly yellow, spotted with brown at the base; lip creamy white.

Pescatorei album.—Large. All pure white.

Pescatorei superbum.—A round flower, of great 'substance'—which means, in effect, that it will last an unusual time. Notable for the deep tone of its purplish markings.

Pescatorei grandiflorum.—Immense. The lip has a yellow dash at base.

Pescatorei splendens.—Sepals and petals white; lip handsomely spotted with purple.

Pescatorei violaceum.—The whole flower is tinted with violet.

Crispum purpureum shows a similar peculiarity, but the tint is purple.

Crispum Dayanum.—The sepals have a large irregular patch of

darkest mauve in the centre, the petals a spot or two of the same colour and a streak at the base. The lip is white.

Old-fashioned people have not yet learned to call Odontoglossum vexillarium a Miltonia. To avoid confusion I will give it no generic name at all. It should be observed, however, that in our collection these plants are 'grown cool' all the year round. Among the most important are:—

Vexillaria Cobbiana.—Pale rose with white lip.

Vexillaria Measuresiana.—All white save the golden 'beard.' Perhaps the handsomest of its rare class.

Vexillaria rubella.—Deep rose. Valuable for its habit of flowering in autumn.

STORY OF ODONTOGLOSSUM HARRYANUM

Men supremely great in science have a quality beyond reason, such as we term instinct, enabling them to leap over the slow processes of demonstration, and announce a law or a result unsuspected, which they cannot yet prove. The great Collector Benedict Roezl had this gift. Returning from the memorable expedition in which he discovered the Miltonia commonly called Odontoglossum vexillarium, he assured Mr. Sander that in those parts would be found a true Odontoglossum of unusual colouring. When asked the grounds for his opinion he could only say he 'smelt it.' Mr. Sander was not unused to this expression, and he knew by experience that Roezl's scientific nose might be trusted. It was something in the air, in the 'lie' of the country, in the type of vegetation, which guided him, no doubt. Other collectors born and bred have a like sense. Roezl showed his supremacy by the confident prediction that this new species would be darker than any known, and striking in the combination of its tints.

This was in 1875. Ten years later Professor Reichenbach wrote to Mr. Sander of an astounding Odontoglossum he had seen—it may be necessary to tell the unlearned that Professor Reichenbach was the very genius of orchidology. Nothing in the least resembling it had been even rumoured hitherto. And then Reichenbach described Odontoglossum Harryanum. The raptures of that enthusiast were wont to divert admiring friends, expressed with quaint vehemence, but always suggesting that he mocked himself the while. Never had he such a theme as this. Speaking with due thought and sufficient knowledge, I declare that Odontoglossum Harryanum is the most finished result of Nature's efforts to produce a flower which should startle and impress by its colours alone, without eccentricity of shape or giant size, or peculiarities of structure. Remembering that not all the world has seen this flower, I should give just a hint of the means employed. Fancy, then, eight or ten great blooms, dark chestnut in tone, barred with yellow, striped with mauve; the lip white, broadly edged with a network of bluish purple and intersected by a deep stain of that tint, beyond which is spread a sheet of snow; touch with gold here and there, and you have the 'scheme of colour.' Those who knew the great savant can imagine how he raved after giving, with luminous precision, his scientific report of the new orchid.

Reichenbach persuaded himself, by study of the flower, that it must be a native of Mexico. He was wrong for once, but people were

152

so used to regard him as infallible that Mr. Sander did not think of doubting the assertion. Presently, however, it became known that Messrs. Veitch had bought the plants, a dozen or so, from Messrs. Horsman. And then Mr. Sander learned by accident that the latter firm received a small case of orchids from Barranquilla, twelve months before. While pondering this news, Roezl's unforgotten prophecy flashed into his mind. Barranquilla, in the United States of Columbia, is the port of that district where Odontoglossum vexillarium is found! He had a collector not far away. Within an hour this gentleman, Mr. Kerbach, received a telegram short and imperative: 'Go Amalfi.' Not waiting an explanation Kerbach replied 'Gone!'—reached Amalfi in due course, and found another telegram containing a hint that sufficed, 'New Odontoglossum.'

Kerbach began to inquire the same day. It was hardly credible that an orchid of importance could have been overlooked in the neighbourhood of Amalfi, where collectors—French, Belgian, and English—had been busy for years. A hunt there would be very unpromising. Kerbach wandered about, asking questions. Thus at Medellin he made acquaintance with a Bank clerk. It may be noted, by the way, that the inhabitants of that busy and thriving town, the bulk of them, are descendants of Maranos—that is, Jews converted by the processes of the Inquisition. Doubtless there are records which explain why and how many thousands of those people assembled in a remote district of New Granada, but they themselves appear to have lost the tradition; they have lost their ancestral faith also, for there are no more devout Catholics. The religious instincts of the race assert themselves, however, for New Granadans in general are not more fervent than other creoles of South America, while the town of Medellin is an oasis of piety.

The Bank clerk was questioned as usual, though not a likely person to take note of plants. 'Why,' said he, 'there was a customer of ours at the Bank yesterday, swearing like a wild Indian at orchids and everybody connected with them. I should advise you to keep out of his way.'

'What have the orchids done to him?' asked Kerbach.

'I wasn't listening, but I'll inquire.' And presently he brought the explanation. A young French collector had been in those parts some years before. He stayed a while at the planter's house, and there discovered an orchid which stirred him to enthusiasm. After gathering a quantity he made arrangements with his host for a shipment to follow next season, promising a sum which astonished the native. But this young man was drowned in the Couca. After a while Don Filipe resolved to despatch a few of the weeds on his own account to Europe, and he consigned them to a friend at

Barranquilla. But the friend never returned him a farthing. He had handed the case to some one else for shipment, and this some one, he said, could not get his money from England. It is pleasant to hear, however, that Don Filipe had implicit trust in British honesty. He proclaimed his friend a swindler, and doubtless he was right.

All the cash that this good man was out of pocket could not well have exceeded ten dollars, and his time did not count. Perhaps he would have been less furious had the loss been greater. Anyhow he nursed his wrath with Indian stubbornness—for Don Filipe was an Indian, though distinguishable from a white only in character, as are myriads at this day.

Kerbach did not doubt that he had found his Odontoglossum, and gaily started for the hacienda. Some little diplomacy might be needed, and rather more cash than usual; but of course a sane man would come to terms at last. Don Filipe was absent when he arrived—a fortunate chance, perhaps. Meantime Kerbach entertained the ladies, played with the children, and made himself agreeable. The haciendero found him seated at the piano, and applauded with the rest.

But his face changed when they got to business. Kerbach opened with flattering remarks upon the wealth of the country and its prospects. Don Filipe purred with satisfaction. Gradually he worked round to orchids. Don Filipe ceased to purr, and he hastily begged leave to visit the cacao plantation. As they rode through the sheltering woods Kerbach looked about him sharply. It was too late for flowers, but the growth of Odontoglossum Harryanum is very distinct. He espied one plant and recognised it as a new species.

The trouble must be faced, and after dinner Kerbach explained his object, as gently as he could. The planter flamed out at once, dropped his Castilian manners, and vowed he would shoot any man found gathering orchids on his estate. Kerbach withdrew. Next day he visited two other hacienderos of the district. But Don Filipe had preceded him. Less rudely but with equal firmness the landowners forbade him to collect on their property.

A brief explanation is needed. In those parts of South America, where the value of orchids is known to every child, a regular system has been introduced long since. As a rule almost invariable, the woods belong to some one, however far from a settlement. With this personage the collector must negotiate a lease, as it is called, a formal document, stamped and registered, which gives him authority to cut down trees—for the peons will not climb. At the beginning, doubtless, they shrewdly perceived that to fell a stout trunk would pay them infinitely better—since they receive a daily wage—than to strip it, besides the annoyance from insects and the risk from snakes which they elude. At the present time this usage has become fixed.[2]

Without the assistance of peons, Kerbach could not possibly get plants sufficient to ship. To cut down trees without authority would be a penal offence, certainly detected. He explored the country at a distance and found nothing. It was necessary to come to terms with Don Filipe at any cost or abandon the enterprise. Meantime letters reached Amalfi describing the new Odontoglossum, with a picture showing the foliage. It was that he had found. The treasure hung within reach, and a pig-headed Indian forbade him to grasp it.

In such a difficulty one applies to the Cura. Kerbach paid this gentleman a visit. A tall, stout, good-natured ecclesiastic was he, willing to help a stranger, perhaps, even though unprovided with the dollars which Kerbach offered 'for the poor,' if his mediation proved successful. The Cura made the attempt and failed signally. It was useless to try again. The good man begged ten dollars, or five, or one, upon the ground that he had done his best. But Kerbach in despair was not inclined for charity. The Cura sighed, hesitated, tossed off a glass of aguardiente and proposed another way.

'This is a wicked country, sir,' he said. 'Ah! very wicked. And the wickedest people in it have a proverb which I shudder to repeat. But your case is hard. Well, sir, they say (heaven forgive them and me!), "If the saints won't hear you, take your prayer to the devil." Horrible, isn't it?'

'Horrible!' said Kerbach. 'But I don't know where to find the devil.'

'Yours is a pious country I have heard, though not Christian. In this wicked land even children could tell you where to seek him. Now, you will give me a trifle for my poor?' And he held out his hand.

'But I'm not acquainted with any children. Your reverence must really be more explicit.'

'Bother!' exclaimed his reverence, or some Spanish equivalent. 'Well, you will pay me the fifty dollars promised?'

'Twenty! When Don Filipe signs the lease.'

'And all incidental expenses? Then my sacristan will call on you to-morrow. Never talk to me again of your impious projects, sir.'

The sacristan was very business-like. He demanded a dollar to begin with for the Indian who would work the charm, and another

---

[2] Two or three years ago, however, the Government of New Granada made a law forbidding such destruction of trees—a measure which has happily reduced the output of orchids, since the natives are unwilling to climb for them.

dollar for himself to pay for the masses which would expiate his sin. Kerbach asked details, which were given quite frankly. The wizard was a respectable person—attended church, and so forth. The sacristan had talked matters over with him and neither doubted of success. Kerbach must write a letter to Don Filipe's wife begging her to intercede. The wizard having charmed that document before presenting it, she would be compelled to grant its request. If the planter should still refuse, a curse would be launched against him. And he could not dare resist that.

The man was so serious, he explained himself in such a matter-of-fact tone, that Kerbach, laughing, risked two dollars on the chance. With the letter in his pocket the sacristan departed. Two days later he returned. Don Filipe was willing to negotiate the lease. Kerbach was so delighted that he never thought of asking whether the lady's gentle influence or the terrors of the curse had persuaded him. Thus Odontoglossum Harryanum was found, to the eternal glory of Roezl.

MASDEVALLIAS

Among Masdevallias we have scarce varieties of Harryana, as Bull's Blood, Mr. Bull's punning name for the darkest of all crimsons, and Denisoniana, which keen eyes distinguish from it by a shade of magenta; splendens, pure magenta; versicolor, which has patches of deep crimson on a magenta ground, and a bright yellow 'eye'; Armeniaca, large, apricot in colour, also with a yellow 'eye'; Sander's Scarlet, which speaks for itself.

Bonplandii.—Greenish yellow, with a few purple marks. Tails short and stiff.

Caudata.—Upper sepal light yellow dotted with red; lower purplish rose, marbled with white. A dwarf species, but the yellow tails are two to three inches long.

Abbreviata.—Small, white speckled with purple.

Ignea splendens.—Much larger than the normal form. Fiery red.

Amabilis.—Small, carmine, conspicuous by reason of its 'tail,' an inch and a half long.

Chelsoni.—A hybrid of the last-named with Veitchii, orange-yellow, with mauve spots and two 'tails.'

Veitchii grandiflora, a variety even larger than the common type, seven inches across sometimes; orange-red, suffused with purple.

Polysticta.—One of the lovely little 'curiosities' which abound in this genus—palest lilac freckled with purple, and tailed.

Coccinea.—Rosy pink above, glowing scarlet below.

Macrura.—One of the few Masdevallias which do not please my eye, but very rare. Immense, as much as twelve inches long, counting the yellow tails, rough of surface, vaguely brown in colour, with darker spots.

Peristeria.—Greenish yellow, freely speckled with purple; yellow-tailed.

Melanopus.—Small, white, dotted with purple and yellow-tailed.

Wallisii stupenda.—-Pale lemon colour splashed with chocolate. There is a curious white excrescence on each side the column, dotted with scarlet.

ONCIDIUMS

Of Oncidiums in this house I note:—

Lamelligerum.—A very grand and noble flower, too rarely seen. It belongs to the stately section of which Oncidium macranthum is the common type. The great dorsal sepal swells out roundly from a stalk half an inch long; the two lower resemble in shape those long-bladed paddles, with scalloped edge, which are used by chiefs in the South Seas; in colour rich brown, with a clear golden margin. The yellow petals also have a stalk, but to give a notion of the large, beautiful, and complex development which they carry at the ends is a hopeless endeavour. I have seen ladies' work-baskets which faintly resemble it when wide open; made of the softest straw, without end-pieces, only to be closed by tying a ribbon in the centre. But really the case is desperate. I pass on.

Tetracopis.—Another of the same group, even more rare, but not so striking. Large, as they all are. Sepals a lively brown, gold edged; petals bright yellow splashed with brown; lip yellow.

Undulatum.—A third member of this handsome family. Sepals brown, petals white, marbled with yellow and mauve at the base, spotted with purple above, and streaked with yellow. Lip very small, as in all the other cases, but conspicuous by reason of its bright purple tint.

Ornithorhynchum album.—This is one of our oldest and commonest species, discovered by Bonpland, who accompanied Humboldt to Mexico; brought to Europe no long time afterwards. But the pure white variety turned up to astonish the world very few years ago, and the names of those happy mortals who possess a sample would make only a brief if distinguished list.

Loxense seems to have been not uncommon in our fathers' time, but no plants have arrived from Peru—Loxa is the district—for many years. It makes a long spike with branches, bearing a great number of large flowers; sepals greenish ochre, crossed with blurs of chocolate; petals deep brown, edged and tipped with yellow. Lip large and flowing, as it were, orange-yellow, speckled with red in the throat.

Weltoni.—-Classed of late among Miltonias. A singular and fascinating species, difficult to grow and still more difficult to flower. The sepals and petals are very narrow, with edges like a saw, greenish brown, widening out suddenly at the tip, which is yellow. The lip is extraordinary in all respects. It shows a fine broad disc of dusky purple, with a darker bar across the middle; and below this, sharply divided as if by a stroke of the brush, two smaller discs pure white. Upon the whole to be wondered at rather than admired, but more interesting on that account.

STORY OF ONCIDIUM SPLENDIDUM

We all know that to make a thing conspicuous above measure is the most effective way of baffling those who seek it. Wendell Holmes has expounded the natural law of this phenomenon, and Edgar Poe exemplified it in a famous story. I am about to give an instance from the life, as striking as his fiction.

Oncidium splendidum is one of the stateliest orchids we have, and one of the showiest. Its leaves are very large, fleshy and rigid, and the tall flower spike bears a number of pale yellow blooms striped with brown, each three inches across. There is no exaggeration in saving that they would catch the most careless eye as far off as one could see them.

At an uncertain date in the fifties a merchant captain—whose name and that of his ship have never been recovered—brought half a dozen specimens to St. Lazare and gave them to his owner, M. Herman. This gentleman sold the lot to MM. Thibaud and Ketteler, orchid-dealers of Sceaux. They were tempted to divide plants so striking and so new; thus a number of small and weakly pieces were distributed about Europe at a prodigious price. We have the record of the sale of one at Stevens' Auction Rooms in 1870; it could show but a single leaf, yet somebody paid thirty guineas for the morsel. So ruthlessly were the plants cut up. Even orchids, tenacious of life as they are, will not stand this treatment. In very few years more Oncidium splendidum had vanished.

No one knew where it came from—with a strange carelessness MM. Thibaud and Ketteler had not inquired. M. Herman was dead, and he left no record of the circumstances. The captain could not be traced. Had the name of his ship been preserved, it might have furnished a hint, since the port of sailing would be registered in the Custom House. More than one enterprising dealer made inquiries, but it was too late to recover the trail. Oncidium splendidum took its place for a while among the lost orchids.

But Mr. Sander of St. Albans would not admit defeat. When, after great pains, he had satisfied himself that nothing could be discovered at St. Lazare or at Sceaux, he examined the internal evidence. In the first place, an Oncidium must needs be American, since the genus is not found in the Old World. This species also must dwell in a hot climate; leaves so rigid and fleshy are designed to bear a scorching sun. But the possibilities seemed almost boundless, even thus limited. Patiently and thoughtfully Mr. Sander worked out a process of exhaustion. Mexico might be neglected, for

160

a time at least; those hunting-grounds had been so often explored that some one must surely have come across a flower so conspicuous. So it was with New Grenada. Brazilian Cattleyas have thick, hard leaves, though not to compare with this Oncidium; but they form a single genus which shows the peculiarity among hundreds which do not. Brazil, therefore, might be excluded for the present. The astonishing wealth of Peru in varieties of orchid was not suspected then. After such careful thought as a man of business allows himself when tempted by a speculation which may cost thousands of pounds, Mr. Sander determined that, upon the whole, Central America was the most likely spot; and again, after more balancing of the chances, that Costa Rica was the most likely part of Central America.

After coming to a decision he acted promptly. In 1878 Mr. Oversluys, one of our trustiest and most experienced collectors, was despatched to Costa Rica. More than three years he travelled up and down, and treasures new or old he sent in abundance—Epidendron ciliare, Cattleya Bowringiana, Oncidium cheirophorum, are names that occur at the moment. But as for Oncidium splendidum he had not so much as heard of it. Not a peon could be found in the woods to recognise the sketch which Mr. Sander had given him. Oversluys had never seen the plant himself, I think.

He was driven at length to conclude that if the thing did really exist in those parts—poor Oversluys applied a variety of epithets to 'the thing' now, none expressive of tenderness—it must be on the Atlantic slope or the steaming lowlands beyond. He had felt himself justified in neglecting those districts hitherto because there is no port where a large vessel can lie, and absolutely no trade, save a trifling export of bananas. What could tempt a French captain to the Atlantic shore of Costa Rica? And the expedition was as uninviting as well could be. There were no towns nor even villages—but it must be borne in mind that I speak of twenty years ago. At that time all the white and coloured population was settled on the tableland, excepting a few individuals or families who yearly wandered downwards to squat along the slope. Upon the other hand there were Indian tribes—Talamancas to the southward, who admitted some vague allegiance to the Republic on condition that white men did not enter their territory; and Guatusos or Pranzos to the northward, utter savages. It was their country, however, to which the wandering folks mentioned betook themselves, and thither Oversluys must go; for the track they had cut through the forest was the only one connecting the tableland with the Atlantic coast.

I have travelled that 'road' myself in the days when peril and discomfort were welcome for the promise of adventure; but had we

161

known what lay before us when bidding a joyous adieu to the capital, we should have meekly returned to the Pacific harbour by coach. Oversluys was a man of business, and to men of business adventure commonly means embarrassment and loss of time, if no worse. Varied experiences, all unpleasant, told him that to seek orchids in a country like that must be a thankless enterprise, attended by annoyance, privation, and even danger. But he had undertaken the work. It must be done.

As cheerfully then as such untoward circumstances permitted, Oversluys set forth from San José, and in due time reached the Disengagno. This is a blockhouse raised by some charitable person on the edge of the tableland; a very few yards beyond, the path dips suddenly on its course to the Serebpiqui river, 6000 feet below. The spot is bitterly cold at night, as I can testify, or seems so, and for this reason the hut was built, as a shelter for travellers. But they, too lazy to seek wood in the forest at arm's length, promptly demolished the walls and burned them. Only the roof remained in a few months, with the posts that upheld it.

A group of ill-looking peons occupied this shed when Oversluys arrived. They began to pick a quarrel forthwith; in short, he heartily wished himself elsewhere. It was not yet dusk. Drawing the guide apart Oversluys questioned him, and learned that there was one single habitation within reach. The report of it was not promising, but he did not hesitate. As the little party filed off, one of the peons shouted, 'A good night, macho! We'll wait for you at La Vergen!'— the first halting-place on the descent. A pleasant beginning!

The shelter they sought lay some miles back. There is plenty of game on these unpeopled uplands, if a man knows how to find it, and a hunter had built himself this cabin in the woods. They reached it as darkness was setting in—a hut as rough as could be, standing on the edge of a small savannah. At the same moment the owner returned, with a deer tied on the back of a small but very pretty ox. He might well be surprised, but hospitality is a thing of course in those parts. Kindness to animals is not, however—much the contrary—and Oversluys observed with pleasure how carefully the little ox was treated. Children came running from the hut, and, after staring in dumb amaze for a while at the strangers, took the animal and actually groomed it in a rough way.

After supper—of venison steaks—Oversluys alluded to this extraordinary proceeding. The guide said, 'Our friend Pablo may well take care of his ox. There's not such another for hunting on the countryside.' And Pablo grunted acquiescence.

'For hunting?' asked Oversluys.

162

'Yes. You should see him when he catches sight of deer. Tell the gentleman, Pablo.'

Upon this theme the hunter was talkative, and he reported such instances of sagacity that Oversluys—remembering those ruffians who awaited him at La Vergen—asked whether there was any chance to see the ox at work? Pablo meant to have another stalk at dawn, with the hope of carrying two deer to market, and willingly he agreed to take his guest. So they started before daylight.

It was no long journey to the hunting-ground. These high lands are mostly savannah, with belts of dense forest between. Oversluys had heard deer belling incessantly all night. After carefully studying the wind Pablo chose the direction of the hunt. He had cut tracks to each point of the compass, and he took that which would bring him to the edge of the first clearing with the wind in his face.

It was just light enough when they arrived to see half a dozen dark forms above the misty grass. Forthwith Pablo crept out from the trees, walking backwards, his left arm round the ox's neck, and his stooped body behind its shoulder. Thus he could see nothing. It was unnecessary. The ox marched on, its broadside towards the deer, very softly, but always zigzagging closer. As the light strengthened, Oversluys watched with growing pleasure. Very soon the deer noticed this intrusion and ceased feeding; then the ox dropped its head and grazed. Again and again this occurred. So long as one deer remained upon the watch it kept its head down, but when the last recovered confidence, instantly it advanced. Pablo's old gun could not be trusted beyond fifty yards or so. The deer became more restless. They drew together—Oversluys saw they would bound off in a moment. Just then the ox wheeled actively— they flew. But one rolled over, shot through the chest.

Oversluys was so pleasantly excited that he ran to pat the clever creature. Then he assisted Pablo to load up the game. It was broad daylight now. In lifting the body he noticed some large yellow flowers which it had crushed in falling. They were pretty and curious in shape. He glanced at the leaves—they were large, polished, and very stiff. A wild fancy struck him. He compared the drawing. There was no doubt! Scores of Oncidium splendidum starred the tall grass all around!

I do not try to paint his raptures. A few weeks later many thousand plants were on their way to Europe. But the point of the story is that Mr. Oversluys had seen and even admired this flower many a time on the upland savannahs in riding past. He was looking for orchids, however, and who could have expected to find an Oncidium buried among herbage in the open ground?

The ox demands a word. Such trained animals are not

uncommon in Central America. The process of education is very cruel. By constant tapping, their horns are loosened when young, so that the tortured beast obeys the slightest pressure. Its movements in walking are thus directed, and when the horns grow firm again it continues to recognise a touch. But the degrees of intelligence in brutes are strikingly displayed here. Some forget the lesson in a twelvemonth. Most are uncertain. A very few, like Pablo's, understand so well what is required of them that direction is needless. In that case the hunter can walk backwards, keeping his body quite concealed. He is almost sure to kill, unless the fault be his own.

LAELIA JONGHEANA

The back wall carries a broad sloping ledge of tufa, where little chips of Odontoglossum and the rest are planted out to grow until they become large enough to be potted—no long time, for they gather strength fast in niches of the porous stone. Along the top, however, are ranged flowering plants of Odontoglossum grande which make a blaze in their season—three to six blooms upon a spike, the smallest of them four inches across. Overhead is a long row of Laelia Jongheana—some three hundred of them here and elsewhere. It is a species with a history, and I venture to transcribe the account which I published in the Pall Mall Gazette, July 18, 1899.

'A Sensation for the Elect.—The general public will hear without emotion that Laelia Jongheana has been rediscovered. The name is vaguely suggestive of orchids—things delightful in a show, or indeed elsewhere, when in bloom, but not exhilarating to read about. Therefore I call the news a sensation for the elect. At the present moment, I believe, only one plant of L. Jongheana is established in this country, among Baron Schröder's wonders. Though its history is lost this must be a lonely survivor of those which reached Europe in 1855—a generation and a half ago. It is not to be alleged that no civilised mortal has beheld the precious weed in its native forests since that date; but no one has mentioned the spectacle, and assuredly no one has troubled to gather plants. Registered long since among the "Lost Orchids," which should bring a little fortune to the discoverer, native botanists and dealers in all parts of South America have been looking out. And the collectors! For forty years past not one of the multitude has left the shores of Europe or the United States, bound for the Cattleya realm, without special instructions to watch and pray for L. Jongheana. More and more pressing grew the exhortations as years went by and prices mounted higher, until of late they subsided in despair. Yet the flower is almost conspicuous enough to be a landmark, and it does not hide in the tree-tops either, like so many.

'Every one who takes interest in orchids will be prepared already to hear that Messrs. Sander are the men of fate. How many of such spells have they broken! Without book I recall Oncidium splendidum, of which not a plant remained in Europe, nor a hint of the country where it grew; the "scarlet Phalaenopsis" of native legend, never beheld of white man, which, in fact, proved to be brick-red; Cattleya labiata, the Lost Orchid par excellence, vainly sought from 1818 to 1889. The recovery of Dendrobium Schröderium was chronicled by every daily paper in London, or almost, with a leader, when a skull was shown in Protheroe's Rooms with a specimen clinging to it, and a select group of idols accompanying the shipment. Less important, but not less interesting, was the reappearance of Cypripedium Marstersianum at a later date. Verily, we orchidists owe a debt to the St. Albans firm.

'In these cases success was merited by hard thought, patient inquiry, and long effort. Working out the problem in his study, Mr. Sander fixed upon a certain country where the prize would be found, and sent his collector to the spot. Oversluys searched for Oncidium splendidum during three years, until he wrote home that it might be in —— or ——, but it certainly was not in Costa Rica; yet he found it at last. In this present case, however, the discovery is due to pure luck; but one may say that a slice of luck also was well deserved after those laborious triumphs. One of the St. Albans collectors, M. Forget, was roaming about Brazil lately. The Government invited him to join a scientific mission setting out to study the products and resources of Minas Gaeras. It is comparatively little known. M. Forget was unable to accept the invitation, but he heard enough about this secluded province to rouse his interest, especially when the savants reported that no collector had been there. Accordingly, he made an expedition as soon as possible, and at the very outset discovered an orchid—not in flower—resembling Laelia pumila in every detail but size. It was at least twice as big as that small, familiar species, but the points of similarity were so striking that M. Forget pronounced it a grand local form of L. pumila. And when the consignment reached St. Albans, even the wary and thoughtful authorities there endorsed his view! Not without hesitation. I believe that the name of L. Jongheana was whispered. But despair had grown to the pitch that no one ventured to speak out. Yet by drawings and descriptions, anxiously studied for years, all knew perfectly well that in growth the lost species must be like L. pumila, enlarged. It is, indeed, strong evidence of the absorbing interest of the search that when at length it ended, neither M. Forget nor his employers dared to believe their own eyes.

'So in November last year some hundreds or thousands of a remarkable orchid were offered at Protheroe's under the title "L. pumila (?)." Nearly all the leading amateurs and growers bought, I think, but at a very cheap rate. Half a crown apiece would be a liberal average for plants over which millionaires would have battled had they known. But, after all, the luck of the purchasers was not unqualified. Many who read this will feel a dreary satisfaction in learning that if their plants have perished or dwindled, plenty of others are in like case. Further experience shows that they were gathered at the wrong time; of course they reached Europe at the wrong time. And nearly every one put them into heat, which was a final error. L. Jongheana is quite a cool species. Through these accumulated misfortunes only two out of the multitude have flowered up to this, so far as I can hear. The dullest of mortals can feel something of the delicious anxiety of those gentlemen who watched the great bloom swelling from day to day when it began to show its tints, and they proved to be quite unlike those of L. pumila. At length it opened, and L. Jongheana was recovered.

'What sort of a thing is it, after all? For an unlearned description, I should say that the flowers—two, three, or even five in number—are from four to five inches across—sepals, petals, and curl of lip bright amethyst, yellow throat, white centre; the crisped and frilled margin all round suffused with purple. It was discovered in 1855 by Libon, who died soon after, carrying his secret with him. He was sent out by M. de Jonghe, of Brussels—hence the name.'

Up to the present time only one of the plants here has flowered—and it opened pure white, saving a yellow stain on the lip. This was not altogether a surprise, for a close examination of the faded blooms convinced M. Forget that some of them must have been white, whatever the species might be. And he marked them accordingly. That a collector of such experience should prove to be right was not astonishing, as I say, but remarkably pleasant.

At the end of the house is a pretty verdant nook where Cypripedium insigne is planted out upon banks of tufa among Adiantums and overshadowing palms.

STORY OF BULBOPHYLLUM BARBIGERUM

This species is so rare in Europe that I must give a word of description. The genus contains the largest and perhaps the smallest of orchids—B. Beccarii, whose stem is six inches in diameter, carrying leaves two feet long, and B. pygmaeum of New Zealand. They are all fly-catchers, I think, equipped with apparatus to trap their prey, as droll commonly in the working as ingenious in the design. Barbigerum has pseudo-bulbs less than an inch high, and its flowers are proportionate. But charm and size are no way akin. Fascination dwells in the lip, which, hanging upon the slenderest possible connection, lengthens out to the semblance of a brush. Thus exquisitely poised it rocks without ceasing, and its long, silky, purple-brown hairs wave softly but steadily all day long, as if on the back of a moving insect. Pretty though it be, all declare it uncanny.

The species was introduced from Sierra Leone by Messrs. Loddiges, so long ago as 1835. I have not come upon any reference to a public sensation. Assuredly, however, the orchidists of the day were struck, and it is probable that Messrs. Loddiges sold the wonder at a high price if in bloom. Some people in Sierra Leone forwarded consignments. But an orchid so small and delicate needs careful handling. None of them reached Europe alive, I dare say.

It appears, however, that Bulbophyllum barbigerum is common throughout those regions. The example at Kew, which diverts so many good folks year by year, came from Lagos, near a thousand miles east and south of Sierra Leone. And the story I have to tell places it at Whydah, between the two.

A young man named Boville went thither as clerk in the English factory, soon after 1835. We have not to ask what was his line of commerce. I have no information, but it must be feared, though perhaps we do him wrong, that one branch of it at least was the slave trade. Boville had heard of Messrs. Loddiges' success. Residents at Whydah do not commonly explore the bush, but he was young and enterprising. On his first stroll he discovered the Bulbophyllum, and to his innocence it seemed the promise of a fortune. Real good things must be kept quiet. The treasure was plentiful enough to cause 'a glut' forthwith if many speculators engaged. Luckily he had a Kroo boy in attendance, not a native. To him Boville assumed an air of mystery, said he was going to make fetich, and 'something happen' to any one who spoke of his proceedings—'make fetich' and 'something happen' are among the first local expressions which a man learns in West Africa. The Kroo boy grinned, because that is his way of acknowledging any communication whatsoever, and snapped his fingers in sign of willing obedience. So Boville gathered a dozen plants, and hoped to have a stock before 'the ship' arrived. There were no steamers then, and at Whydah, a very unimportant station for lawful trade, English vessels only called once in three months. Slavers did not ship orchids.

It was Boville's employment henceforth to collect the Bulbophyllum whenever he had a few hours to spare. He hung his spoils on the lattice work which surrounds a bedroom in those parts, between roof and wall, designed for ventilation—hiding them with clothes and things. It is proper to add that the 'English Fort' was already deserted, and the 'Factory' a mere name. The agent, his superior officer, was not at all likely to visit a clerk's quarters. This good man belonged to a class very frequent then upon 'the coast.' He had not returned to England, nor wished to do so, since coming out. At a glance he recognised that this was his real native land, and without difficulty he made himself a fellow-countryman of the negroes, living like a caboceer, amidst an undeterminate number of wives, slaves, and children. Very shocking; but it may be pointed out that such men as this established our colonies or seats of trade in Africa. They had virtues, perhaps, but their vices were more useful. The moral system of the present day would not have answered then. An agent secured his position by marrying a daughter of every chief who might be troublesome. He had no Maxim guns.

Mr. Blank knew every feeling and superstition of the negroes,— that is the point of my reference to his character. And one evening he entered the room just as Boville was hanging up his latest acquisitions, some of which were in flower. Whatever Mr. Blank's business, it fled from his mind on beholding the orchids.

'Good God!' he cried. 'What—what—you are no better than a dead man! I won't protect you—I can't! Good God! What possessed you?'

'I don't understand,' said Boville.

'No, you don't understand! They send me out the most infernal idiots'—and then Mr. Blank fell to swearing.

Boville saw the case was grave somehow. 'Are they poisonous?' he asked.

'Poisonous be—etc. etc. That's the Endua—the holiest of plants! You'll wish they were poisonous before long! What a lot! You didn't get 'em all to-day?'

'I can destroy them. Only Georgius Rex the Krooman has been into the bush with me.'

169

'You fool! D'you think you can hide this from the fetich? Put—put 'em in a sack, and tumble 'em into the river after dark! Oh Lord, here's an awful business!'

Moving about the room restlessly as he talked, whilst Boville thrust the orchids into a bag, the agent opened a door which gave upon a platform called the verandah—in fact, the roof of the store. It overlooked the street. In an instant he ran back.

'It's all up' he cried. 'Oh Lord! Here's the Vokhimen!'

Boville had heard this name, which belongs to an official of the Vo-dun, the fetich priesthood, whose duty it is to summon offenders. He went to see. The street was in an uproar. Two men clothed in black and white, with faces chalked, were beating Vo-drums furiously—but such din is too usual for notice. They stood at the door of a house—habitations in Whydah are not properly described as huts. All the neighbours surged round vociferous. Presently emerged a grotesque figure, rather clothed than adorned with strings of human teeth and bones, and little wooden idols painted red. His black and white cap had lappets with red snakes sewn thereon; the breast of his tunic bore a large red cross, the sacred symbol of Dahomey. He came forth with a leap, and danced along with ridiculous gestures to the next house, flourishing the iron bar which marks his office. The bones and images rattled like castanets. The drummers followed. Through the next doorway the Vokhimen sprang, and disappeared.

'He isn't after me, thank God!' cried Boville.

'He is, you fool! It's their way to hunt about like that when they well know where to find the victim. No, it's too late to hide the cursed things now. God help you, Boville! I can do nothing.' And Mr. Blank hurried out.

'Go to the Hun-to at least, sir—and to Mr. Martinez! Don't leave me helpless to these devils!'

'I'll do all I can for you, but it's worse than useless my stopping here.'

Perhaps it is necessary to observe that the Europeans in Whydah had long been subject to the King of Dahomey, ruled by a Viceroy. Each nationality had its official chief, called Hun-to by the English, and the Portuguese representative enjoyed particular consideration. Nevertheless, the Viceroy was their absolute master, and he obeyed the fetich men.

It is so easy to conceive poor Boville's bewilderment and despair that I shall not dwell upon the situation. With feverish haste he concealed his orchids. Mr. Blank reappeared, with a rope fringed with strips of palm leaf, dry and crackling. This he threw round Boville's neck.

170

'They daren't hurt you with that on!' he cried. 'Only the head priest can remove it! Go down! I've set drink on the table! Good-bye!'

The poor fellow obeyed, taking a pistol. All the servants were clustered at the door, wide-eyed, humming with terror and excitement. Presently the drums sounded nearer and nearer—the throng opened—the Vokhimen danced through, jibbering, curveting, posturing. He started at sight of the palm-leaf cord, but passed by, unheeding a glass of rum which Boville offered, and pranced upstairs. The agent was right. This devil knew where to look! He thumped about a while overhead, then capered down, with a bundle of orchids dangling on the iron stick. The glass was not refused this time. After drinking, the summoner touched Boville with his wand of office, saying, 'Come! The snake calls you!'

Boville did not understand the formula, but he guessed its meaning. There was no help. He set forth. The Vokhimen pocketed the rum bottle and followed, moving gravely enough now.

The mob shouted with astonishment at the appearance of a white criminal, but when the cause of his arrest was seen—that bundle of the holy Endua—astonishment changed to rage. Boville owed his life to the Azan, the fetich cord, at that instant. But the drummers beat furiously, and, as if in response, a dozen fetich men suddenly appeared, pushing through the crowd. One side of their heads was shaven bare. They wore garments of hideous fantasy, charms and horrid objects innumerable, and each a pair of silver horns upon the forehead. Under this escort Boville marched to the fetich place.

This was a bare piece of ground, encircled by the low dark dwellings of the priests, with the sacred wood behind it, and in the midst the Snake Temple. Often had Boville glanced into the small building, which has no door, and seen the reptiles swarming inside. He did not feel the loathing for snakes which is so common— happily, as it proved. But no man could watch that multitude of restless, twining creatures without horror.

Led to the dreadful doorway, Boville turned, thinking to resist; but they fell upon him, doubled him up—for the entrance was very low—and thrust him in bodily. The poor fellow screamed in tumbling full length upon a platform which occupied the middle. He had seen it alive with snakes, writhing one over the other.

But none were there. He scrambled to his feet and looked round. The temple had no windows, but the solid walls of adobe did not meet the roof, and the level sun-rays of evening poured through the gap. There was nothing to interrupt the view, save a besom and

171

a basket. But no snake could he see. A movement above caught his eye. He looked up.

There are men who would have lost their wits in terror at that sight. The snakes were there, hundreds of them, perched upon the thickness of the wall—the ridge of their bodies gleaming in the red light of sunset, their long necks hanging down, waving and twining. Every head was turned towards him, the glass-bright eyes fixed on his, and the tongues slithering with eagerness. Nightmare was never so horrible.

For an instant Boville stood frozen, with dropped jaw and starting eyes, the icy sweat streaming from every pore; then, howling in no human voice, he burst through the doorway, through the guard, and fell in the midst of a party advancing.

All the Europeans in Whydah were there, with the Viceroy himself, and the head fetich man. The horrid absurdity of their equipment I have no room to describe. The white men had been pleading, even threatening, and the Viceroy supported them. When Boville dropped at their feet the last word had been spoken. His punishment should be that decreed against the man who kills a snake by evil chance—no worse.

'What is that?' Boville panted, when the agent who held him in his arms had explained.

'Never mind—we'll do our best! And it is to be at once, thank God! Night will soon be here!'

'Don't go—not all of you! Don't leave me with these devils!'

'We must, poor boy—to arrange. But we shall return.'

Boville remained among a group of fetich men, who sang and capered round, making gruesome pantomime of tortures. Meanwhile, others were busy at a shed with spades and bundles of reed. Dusk was settling down when they had finished. The head priests returning took their stations, surrounded by men with torches still unlit. All the population was gathered round the holy area.

Mr. Blank came back with others. 'Listen,' he said. 'They are going to put you—unbound—in a hole, cover you with reeds, and set them alight. You must spring up and run to the nearest water, all these brutes after you. But I have arranged with many of them, and they will intercept the others. Now mark, for your life may depend on it! The law is that one who kills a snake shall be cut and hacked till he reaches water! They expect you to make for the river, but there is a pond on the very edge of the fetich wood yonder! See? You make for that! You can't miss it if you go straight between the torches and the temple. You understand? Now summon your courage, man, and run for your life.'

172

He wrung Boville's hand. The executioners seized their victim and hurried him to the shed, amidst a furious tumult—roaring, singing, beating of drums, and blaring of cow-horns—thrust him into the hole, and heaped combustibles over him. The instant he was free Boville sprang up, but the reeds flared as quick as gunpowder. All ablaze he ran—the savage crew pursuing. But they mostly expected him on the river side. With but little hurt, save burns, he reached the pool and leapt in.

It is satisfactory to add that Boville did not suffer in health or fortune by this dread experience. He became the richest trader in Whydah, a special favourite with the natives. But he collected no more orchids.

THE END

www.ingramcontent.com/pod-product-compliance
Lightning Source LLC
LaVergne TN
LVHW030633080426
835509LV00022B/3458